THE BEGINNING OF THE
ENGLISH REFORMATION

THE
BEGINNING
OF THE
ENGLISH
REFORMATION

by Hugh Ross Williamson

SHEED AND WARD · NEW YORK

To Gordon Wheeler

CONTENTS

THE BEGINNING OF THE
ENGLISH REFORMATION

INTRODUCTION

INTRODUCTION

What It Was

The Reformation has been well defined as a sixteenth-century movement which, while ostensibly directed towards the spiritual renewal of the Church, was in fact a revolt against it and led to the abandonment by the Reformers of essential Christian doctrines. The causes of the Reformation, like those of the fall of the Roman Empire or the outbreak of the French Revolution, provide endless opportunities for neat theses and provoke interminable, if inconclusive, academic arguments.

Catholic historians have themselves admitted and even emphasized that among these causes were the wordliness of many high ecclesiastics, striving for political power and privilege, and, in particular, the appalling state, in this respect, of the Papal Curia; the idleness, superstition, ignorance and indifference of many Christians, including the religious as well as the secular priests; the

3

diminution of the prestige of the Holy See by the Babylonish Captivity and the Great Schism, which accustomed men, during the fourteenth and fifteenth centuries, to underestimate, if not wholly to ignore, the universal and unique character of the Papacy; the organizational concentration of administrative affairs at Rome, with the resultant delay and expense, which exasperated increasingly powerful national interests; and the impact of Renaissance humanism on Christendom in general and the Papacy in particular. This case has been vividly stated by Karl Adam in the opening pages of *The Roots of the Reformation.*

Yet true though these things are, there is another aspect of the truth which must be kept in mind if the perspective is not to become distorted and history "read backwards" with an undue deference to later Protestant propaganda. The Church, as far as the human element goes, has always needed reform, though it has seldom fallen to the level which St. Paul denounced in the apostolic Church at Corinth; the proportion of traitors in the Christian ranks has probably remained in the apostolic ratio of one in twelve and the collective Judas through the ages has been no less active than the individual "son of perdition" was; and the "anti-clericalism" which is at all levels the lever for discontent is a persistent phenomenon, arising from the nature of society, and is not even confined to Christianity. To be "agin" the powers

that be—ecclesiastical, or political, or even cultural—
is a universal human tendency; elements both unhealthy
and healthy are complicatedly combined in it, and
although this study affords neither scope nor occasion
for analyzing its significance, it can at least be said that
anti-clericalism in the ordinary sense is, in part at any
rate, simply one particular manifestation of it.

The decisive factor, at any point in history, is not
conditions but men's reaction to those conditions. The
state of affairs, moral, political, ecclesiastical and social,
against which St. Teresa of Avila had to struggle in her
efforts for reform was no different from that which faced
Luther; but she is one of the greatest of saints and he
one of the most dangerous of heresiarchs precisely because she saw and accepted (which he did not) the
ultimate irrelevance of those conditions to the central
truth that, whatever the failings of the human element,
the Church is the Mystical Body of Christ. To St. Catherine of Siena, the Babylonish Captivity, which oppressed
her spirit with its horror, was not primarily a subject for
theological denunciations but an opportunity to fetch the
Pope back from Avignon. And in England it was St. John
Fisher who said: "If the Pope will not reform the Curia
God will find the means to do it for him" and St. Thomas
More who wrote *Utopia*. Always the true reformers are
the great saints and the measure of the Church's peren-

nial need for reformation is their sanctity and their vision.

Thus, in England, the Protestant triumph was made possible by the failure of Tudor Catholics to fulfil their faith. Three sentences will serve for epitome. St. John Fisher said of his fellow bishops: "The fort is betrayed even of them which should have defended it." St. Thomas More described the English priests as "a weak clergy lacking grace constantly to stand to their learning." And for the laity the Duke of Bedford may be spokesman when he refused to return the plundered property of the Church but threw his rosary into the fire saying that, much as he loved it, he loved his "sweet Abbey of Woburn" more.

The Reformation in England was made possible by the existence of fear, weakness and self-seeking in the very places, where, above all, one might have expected courage, strength and loyalty. No estimate of it which denies or minimizes this can pretend to accuracy.

But, having admitted it, one must admit also that the men of the time had the excuse that originally the religious issue was not as clear-cut as it became later or as it appears to posterity. For there was no immediate doctrinal cleavage. The Reformation in England differs radically from that in Germany. Henry VIII was no Luther. The divorce of the Queen had no connection with the theses at Wittenberg. The Church in England was not corrupt, though it was certainly in need of reorganization, and as far as "reform" was genuine, it was a Catholic organizational reform, as for instance in the matter of Wolsey's attitude to small, understaffed monasteries. Heresy, though it existed, was small in numbers and practically negligible in influence, and there was no popular discontent to fan it. Not for twenty years after the beginning of the Reformation were Protestant doctrines officially adopted, and then they had to be forced on the people by German mercenaries after popular uprisings in fourteen counties. "The one definite thing which can be said about the Reformation in England," writes Sir Maurice Powicke, "is that it was an Act of State."[1] From this unassailable premiss, which today is admitted freely by non-Catholic historians, all the rest proceeds as an inexorable logical necessity. The later doctrinal change was merely an ideological justification for the political and economic revolution which that Act of State deliberately initiated. Practice preceded principles.*

* Non-Catholic readers unfamiliar with the actual time-sequence may find the following epitome of interest. By 1540, the last of the religious houses had been destroyed: in 1541 Henry started to prepare his Primer (the precursor of the Prayer Book) which was issued in 1545, superseding Hindsley's Primer published in 1539. In November 1547, the Chantries Act authorized new spoliations: in April 1548, the Protector Somerset sold (in modern currency) £150,000 worth of his share of them, which sum, according to Professor Pollard, was "an infinitesimal part of the whole" amount realized by the confiscations; in September 1548 Cranmer and the Bishops

A foreign visitor to England at the beginning of the sixteenth century noted that the English were extremely pious. "They all attend Mass every day," he wrote, "and say many *Paternosters* in public. The women carry long rosaries in their hands and any who can read take the Office of Our Lady with them and with some companion recite it in church verse by verse, in a low voice, after the manner of churchmen. On Sunday they always hear Mass in their parish church and give liberal alms."[2] They understood the faith they practised. The circulation

---

started to discuss the preparation of the new Prayer Book embodying the new doctrines. It was only an interim measure, as Cranmer explained to a meeting of foreign Protestants in the April of 1549, "lest excessive changes should repel the people." It was completed and imposed on the country by an Act of Uniformity in December 1549. After the popular rebellion it provoked had been crushed, an order, dated 4 November 1550, was issued for the destruction of all altars, accompanied by letters to bishops giving arguments they should use to reconcile their parishioners to the loss of the ornaments of their churches. In the Convocation of December 1550 and in meetings between Cranmer and the Bishops during the January of 1551, plans were made for the final version of the Prayer Book, which was completed and enforced, by a second Act of Uniformity, in the April of 1552. This marks the moment when, officially, England became Protestant in doctrine—twenty-one years after the beginning of the Reformation and when the economic and political revolution had been carried through to the end. The "propaganda" aspect of the Prayer Book in this matter is discussed later. (See *infra*, pp. 18-23.)

of devotional and instructional books among the popula-
tion of three million may be gauged by the fact that, in
the holocaust of Catholic learning and piety which was
part of the Reformers' policy, a quarter of a million
liturgical books alone were destroyed.[3] The splendour of
the shrines of the saints in England was one of the marvels
of Europe, as pilgrimages to them were part of the social
life of the land. The bare framework of chantries still
to be seen in English cathedrals and churches—a proportion only of the chantries (which were also the schools)
of the land—still bears witness to the piety of those who
left endowments for Masses for souls.

No one can seriously contend that these people pas-
sionately believed that the doctrine of purgatory, the
veneration paid to relics, the invocation of saints and
prayers for the dead were "fond things vainly invented"
and "repugnant to the word of God,"[4] as they were
officially forced to believe after the State had enriched
itself by tens of millions of pounds by destroying the
shrines of the saints and stealing their treasures, and by
pillaging the chantries and confiscating their endowments. On the contrary, the belief in the doctrines had so
manifested itself in the whole texture of the nation's
life and thought, that only the blindest can fail to see
why the State had to attempt to justify, by the importation of a new and convenient theology, a revolution
accurately described by a Protestant historian as "a

sweeping redistribution of wealth, carried out by an unscrupulous minority, using the weapons of violence, intimidation and fraud, and succeeded by an orgy of interested misgovernment on the part of its principal beneficiaries."[5]

This inverted relation of theory to practice is clear enough now. And, once the issue was stated in theological terms, it became clear enough then, as the succession of martyrs bears witness. But at the beginning of it all, in the early 1530's, even good and wise men failed to see that, in matters apparently concerned with such technicalities as the extent of the royal jurisdiction, the payment of ecclesiastical dues and the reorganization of monastic houses, what was at stake was the Catholic faith itself. It took, literally, a saint to see it in all its implications. And, from among the clergy, St. John Fisher, and, from among the laity, St. Thomas More, saw it and died for the vision.

But to the ordinary man and woman, lay or religious, the outward appearance of the Church in relation to the Holy See was, as Henry VII had left it and Henry VIII preserved it in the early years of the reign, calm and even conventional. At the opening of the sixteenth century, in 1501, Henry VII had admitted the papal nuncio who had come to offer indulgences for the Pope's cherished project of a crusade against the Turks (the indulgences were for the faithful who had been unable to attend the previous year's Jubilee in Rome), and the King forwarded the whole of the proceeds—£4000—to Rome, unlike some of his brother-monarchs, who kept half for themselves. Henry additionally integrated the rule of Church and State by appointing only ecclesiastics as his chancellors, and the control of clerical appointments was arranged to the satisfaction of both sides. Chapters were always willing to elect and the Papacy to provide the King's nominees, who were foreigners only when he chose. The Papacy on its part aided Henry in maintaining ordered civil government, by, for example, regulating the rights of sanctuary and, by a statesmanlike Bull confirmed by Alexander VI, ordering traitors in sanctuary to be guarded by royal officers. When there was a clash of the royal and papal authorities—as throughout history everywhere in Europe there inevitably was at times—it was amicably settled, and the earlier statutes of Provisors and Praemunire, passed over a century before, were kept well in the background. The purpose of Provisors was to defeat the Pope's claim to provide the personnel of all English bishoprics, and of Praemunire, to protect the temporal jurisdiction of the King against any wrongful infringement by the Pope. They had been brought into being at the time when the Church was rent by the Babylonish Captivity and the Great Schism. The effect of them then was to make Pope Martin V comment bitterly: "It is not the Pope but the King of England who governs the Church in his dominions"; but their purpose was to safeguard the good government of the Church in England in a time of unpredictable chaos abroad.

In the reign of Henry VII and the early years of his son, it had been demonstrated that national interests were compatible with papal supremacy without any recourse to such legalism, but the limits of the royal power had been also explicitly defined and it was agreed on all sides that "no temporal act can make a temporal man have spiritual jurisdiction"—that the King, for example, could not, of himself, interfere with tithes, since "a temporal act without the assent of the Supreme Head [that is, the Pope] cannot make the King a Parson."

This state of affairs, in which Henry VIII until he wished to "get a divorce" (to use the popular phraseology) enthusiastically concurred, worked admirably. But when the King, for his own reasons, wished to overthrow it, the majority of people might be forgiven if they saw, in its initial stages, nothing more than the reopening of an old political debate, which did not affect the faith.

But from the vantage point of posterity we see that what is called the Reformation in England was accomplished within the span of a lifetime of seventy-five years and that the first definite act of it was in 1531 when the English bishops acknowledged King Henry

VIII as Supreme Head of the Church in England "as far as the law of Christ allows"—a saving clause which made the innovation look hardly more than a debating-motion. But the end of it was the penal anti-Catholic legislation of 1606 which made the reception of Anglican Holy Communion the prerequisite of holding office in the State, and which imposed an Oath of Allegiance so framed that no Catholic could possibly take it. And what, religiously speaking, had been accomplished by the Reformers in that short space of seventy-five years left no doubt in anyone's mind as to the nature of what, in fact, had happened.

By 1606, throughout the length and breadth of England, no monastery or nunnery or shrine or chantry existed; to say Mass or to attend Mass, to make a convert to Catholicism or to be a convert were all punishable by death; an Oath asserting that the Head of the Church in England was the successor of Henry VIII instead of the successor of St. Peter was obligatory on all persons of whatever rank under the penalty of exclusion from places of trust and from all the liberal professions; Catholics were required not only to attend Protestant churches but to take Communion there, under pain of the confiscation of two-thirds of their property; they were debarred from the legal and medical professions, from the army and the universities, and if they sent their children abroad to be educated as Catholics, their inheritance was taken away from them and given to their Protestant relations, who were encouraged by liberal bribes to inform against them. In England there was no crucifix to be seen or any statue of Christ's Mother in any public place, and that none should remain as private relics in Catholic homes, justices of the peace were given indiscriminate right of search; if any crucifix were there discovered, the figure was to be publicly defaced at the Quarter Sessions.[6]

This is but a part of the transformation, which was enforced by that army of spies, *agents provocateurs*, forgers and torturers that forms so prominent a feature of Elizabethan England. The mainspring of the movement, morever, was still, at the end as at the beginning, property. The religious theory continued to safeguard the secular practice. To return to the Faith might have meant to have to return the loot. An abbey might have become an abbey once more instead of the favourite residence of a Protestant landowner. And it was this secular avarice allied with this secret fear which made and kept England Protestant—a fear that continued till the eve of the eighteenth century when the last counterattack made by the last Catholic king (a convert to the faith) was defeated by foreign invasion and the Crown itself was added to the spoils.

To understand how the mass of the nation was coerced into accepting the change—for the common people were

14

the victims rather than the beneficiaries of the economic revolution—it is probably easiest to look at the analogy of Soviet Russia in our own century. An effective power to enforce obedience and "make examples" of the disobedient; an effective propaganda, unwearying and unceasing, to falsify the past and "explain" the present; a coherent ideology for the satisfaction of intellectuals; a patriotism engendered by representing all diplomatic or military nationalist movements as defensive actions against powerful ideological aggressors; and, above all, an "Iron Curtain" to prevent the dissemination of the truth from outside civilizations—these as effectively prevent a Russian born today from understanding the realities of Russia in 1917 as they prevented an Englishman born in 1571 from knowing what happened in 1531.

Yet though the methods of a police state may be to a certain extent effective internally, whatever the relationship of the revolutionary country to the world outside, it is an enforced isolation which is the most important factor in ensuring success. The Act of State in England had, at the very beginning, to provide a safeguard against outside interference, since it was challenging the basic assumption of contemporary Western civilization—that there was a Spiritual Head above and apart from national, secular interests. The first step in—to use a later terminology—"lowering the Iron Curtain" was the Act in restraint of Appeals which deprived Englishmen of their right to appeal to the international, and internationally recognized, jurisdiction of Rome.

This Act, passed in 1533, is crucial. One Protestant historian has described it as constitutionally "the most important of the sixteenth century if not of any century"[7] and another, in a justly famous passage, has written that its Preamble is "remarkable partly because it manufactured history on an unprecedented scale, but chiefly because it has operated from that day to this as a powerful incentive to the manufacture by others upon some similar lines."[8]

By officially inventing past history, it laid the foundations of the basic myth, still monotonously repeated in textbooks, of a sturdy Imperial race defying a "foreign" Pope; but its short-term effect, immediate and practical, was to cut England off from Christendom. It enforced insularity, and when the generation born in the year of its passing was in its maturity England was no longer "Mary's Dowry" and an integral part of Europe, but the isolated island of Queen Elizabeth, with a new and strange system of belief and worship and a novel pattern of tyranny.

This isolation in its turn dictated the "missionary activity" which is so difficult for non-Catholics to appreciate at its true value. The succession of heroic men who "trod the Via Dolorosa from Douai to Tyburn" were inflamed only by love of souls. The missions were in no sense political, as the Government propaganda machine necessarily insisted that they were. They were as nakedly religious as the missions a millennium earlier.

Just as once the Saxons, in destroying the Roman civilization, had so obliterated the Catholic Church in Britain that the Pope had to send Augustine to preach the faith anew to a pagan *ultima Thule,* so now, a thousand years later, Rome had once again to send her missionary priests to face martyrdom in a lapsed and lost land. The superficial differences between the sixth and sixteenth centuries are obvious enough, yet the sixty years between the defeat and death of King Arthur at Camlan in 537 and St. Augustine's exposition of Christianity before King Ethelbert's court in 597 are not in spirit remote from the interim between the passing of the Act of Appeals in 1533 and Blessed Edmund Campion's defence in 1581 before Queen Elizabeth's court of the religion which Augustine had taught. And as Augustine could have pointed back across the change and the chaos to St. Alban, who had died for Christ in Verulamium, so Campion, about to die for Christ in London, could invoke "all the ancient priests, bishops and kings—all that was once the glory of England, the Island of Saints and the most devoted child of the See of Peter" to bear witness against their "degenerate descendants."[9]

Why It Is Misunderstood

The question of the effectiveness of propaganda must be explored a little further before the realities of the Reformation in England can be understood at all by the non-Catholic; for the long-term effect of it has been almost as deadly as the short-term effect was successful. Though the cruder forms are, fortunately, a thing of the past (it is probably now untrue that "ten thousand men would rise against Popery without being sure whether Popery was a man or a horse"), there still exists a more dangerous because more subtle misunderstanding.

To the great body of devout, God-fearing Anglicans, inheritors of a four-century-old tradition moulded by the Book of Common Prayer and the English Bible, it will seem almost blasphemy to say that, originally, both the Prayer Book and the vernacular translation of the Scriptures were deliberately used to give the necessary propaganda-twist to Christian doctrine. Yet so it was. And because this conditions a contemporary and quite honest Protestant misunderstanding, it is necessary to give at least one example in each case.

When in 597 St. Augustine celebrated Holy Communion at Canterbury on his landing in England, he said certain prayers which had been given their final form a few years previously by Gregory the Great, the Pope who had sent him on his mission. Those prayers, some of which were actually primitive and all of which embodied apostolic doctrine, have remained unaltered from that day to this. This circumstance alone gives a central position in the Christian faith to what is sometimes known as the Great Prayer of the Church, though more usually referred to as the Canon of the Mass.

Throughout the whole of the reign of Henry VIII, these prayers were still said in every church in England as they are still said in every Catholic church throughout the world today. But in 1549, another form was imposed in England by Act of Parliament—the form devised by Cranmer for the Book of Common Prayer. This new form was, like the enforcement of new beliefs about purgatory and the intercession of the saints, necessary to provide a *raison d'être* for Government policy, in so far as its practical details had impinged on the people in the form of the confiscation of the chantry lands and endowments, the pillage of the shrines and the substitution of the authority of the King for the authority of the Pope in spiritual matters.

Thomas Cranmer, Archbishop of Canterbury, in charge of propaganda, realized that to rewrite the Great Prayer with these things in mind was an effective way of clothing the naked policy of pillage in the serviceable garments of religious practice. This he proceeded to do, dividing the Prayer into two parts and making one of them optional, altering the order and the wording, substituting the name of the King for that of the Pope as Head of the Church and excising every reference to prayers for the dead and to the existence of the saints. For, as long as the Great Prayer remained intact and in its original form, it was always possible that the counter-Reformation might start within the ranks of the clergy themselves.

When, in the course of its magnificent definition of the universal Church, priests and people prayed, in the Great Prayer, for "Thy servant, our Pope, our Bishop and all true believers" there was always a danger that they might remember that the successor of St. Peter was not the son of Henry VIII. So Cranmer changed this phrase to "all Christian kings, princes and governors and especially Thy servant Edward our King, that under him we may be godly and quietly governed; and grant unto his whole Council and all that are put in authority under him that they may truly and indifferently minister justice. . . ." The secular was thus explicitly substituted for the spiritual, and Cranmer took additional care to emphasize it further. The Great Prayer implores God "to protect, unite and govern the Holy Catholic Church throughout the world." Cranmer reserved the actual word "govern" exclusively for the King and his deputies, and for the original phrase substituted "inspire continually the universal Church with the spirit of truth, unity and concord"—which, even though Protestant theologians have been at pains to point out that it means the same thing, has in fact (especially by the use of "universal" instead of "Catholic") not quite the same effect.

Cranmer's second necessity was to get rid of any idea of praying for the dead in order to cover the confiscation of the chantry endowments. The Great Prayer, embodying Christian custom from apostolic times, runs: "Be mindful, O Lord, of Thy servants, men and women" (at this point the worshipper's particular dead were remembered quietly by name) "who have gone before us with the Sign of Faith and sleep the sleep of peace. To them, O Lord, and to all who rest in Christ, grant, we beseech Thee, a place of refreshing light and peace." This Cranmer turned into: "We also bless Thy holy name for all Thy servants departed this life in Thy faith and fear, beseeching Thee to give us grace so to follow their good examples that with them we may be partakers of Thy heavenly kingdom"; and, further to destroy its original connotation as a prayer for those in purgatory, he removed it from its original context and placed it at an earlier point in the service.

There remained the saints. The Great Prayer is full of the saints. It emphasizes that the Church is not confined to the "Church Militant here on earth" but also includes the Church Triumphant in Heaven. It insists, in its definition of the Church, that the Blessed Virgin Mary, St. John the Baptist, St. Peter and St. Paul, all the apostles, the great missionaries, the evangelists and the martyrs "and all Thy saints" are an integral part of the actual Church. The treasure lavished on the shrines of the saints was merely the outward sign that ordinary men and women were soaked in this Christian belief. But as the shrines had gone, the belief had to go too, and from the Great Prayer Cranmer erased every mention of a saint, even the Virgin Mary.

There were, of course, dozens of other changes made by which primitive Christian teaching was jettisoned to justify sixteenth-century revolutionary policy, but these three points alone are enough to explain how the "Prayer for the Church Militant" of the Prayer Book was, in intention and framing, less a prayer than a piece of political propaganda. But gradually, with the saying of the Great Prayer—the Canon of the Mass—punishable by death, and non-attendance at the saying of the liturgy containing the "Prayer for the Church Militant" punished by crippling fines, the new composition became popularly accepted as normative. And, by the nineteenth century, its doctrine was universally regarded in England, except by a handful of cranks and papists, as the "primitive Christian teaching" faithfully preserved by an Established Church which was "the true Catholic Church in England."

When, in 1874, Archibald Campbell Tait, Archbishop of Canterbury, introduced a Public Worship Regulation Act, directed against those followers of Newman and Pusey who were trying to reintroduce the silent use of the Great Prayer, he described that Prayer as containing "the worst errors of one branch of the Christian Church," and opined that if the congregation knew that the minister was "invoking the prayers of the Blessed Virgin Mary on behalf of the worshippers present," they would "rise and leave the church," and he called upon all Anglicans "to come forward and declare them-·selves manfully against such a desecration of Holy Communion."[10]

Such was the long-term effect of the Reformers' propaganda. And if Tait's ignorance of elementary facts of theology and history may be excused on the grounds that he was speaking, after all, eighty years ago, one has to remember the utterance of the present Archbishop of Canterbury as recently as 1951, speaking as Head of the Anglican Communion: "We have no doctrine of our own—we only possess the Catholic doctrine of the Catholic Church enshrined in the Catholic Creeds."[11]

As long as it is possible for such statements to be made and believed in good faith, so long must one despair of Protestant understanding of the Reformation. It is like trying to explain the workings of the Fire Brigade to a man who is immovably convinced that it exists for the purpose of kindling fires.

The dilemma can be seen even more clearly in the matter of the translation of the Bible. Here knowledge was poisoned at its source. Tyndale, in his version, chose his words with care. The word meaning "idols" he rendered by "images" and thereby "forged a useful tool against the Catholic cultus of the saints and the sacred humanity of Christ." "Confess," which might suggest the sacrament of penance, became "acknowledge." The great key words of the Gospel, "grace" and "salvation" became "favour" and "health."

Even more important to eradicate, from a practical point of view, was the idea of the priesthood and the Visible Church. Here Tyndale (and Cranmer, following him) showed a perception little short of genius. "Priest" was turned into "elder" and "church" became "congregation." So, to take one example, in the Epistle of James, the apostolic advice: "Is any man sick among you? Let him bring in the priests of the church and let them pray over him, anointing him with oil in the name of the Lord," with its obvious reference to the sacrament of unction, could not be allowed to stand. Even Wyclif, in his earlier translation of the Bible, had not tampered with this and had correctly translated "priests of the church." But in Tyndale's version and Cranmer's version, they became "elders of the congregation."[12]

The Reformers could thus appeal to the Bible in the vulgar tongue to bear witness that Holy Writ contained no references to justify contemporary Catholic teaching on and practice of the doctrines in dispute; and when such tendentious mistranslations of the Bible were, quite properly, seized and suppressed by Catholic authorities, Catholics could be additionally accused of "trying to prevent people from reading the Bible." It was as simple as that. And the effectiveness of the double lie was so complete that its echoes still reverberate.

One other example may be given. The Reformers extracted from the Books of the Old Testament certain writings, including the Book of Wisdom and the Books of the Maccabees, to which they gave the name—itself misleading—of "the Apocrypha." In deliberate opposition to the teaching of the Church, they declared that, though these books might be read for edification, yet they do not "establish any doctrine." The segregation meant that, though the great passage in the Epistle to the Hebrews about the succession of martyrs and heroes —"who by faith conquered kingdoms, wrought justice, obtained promises, stopped the mouth of lions, quenched the violence of fire, escaped the edge of the sword, recovered strength from weakness, became valiant in battle, put to flight the armies of foreigners"—was, of course, retained, the chronicle of some of these heroic acts as recorded in another part of the Bible, the Second Book of Maccabees, was not.

Nor was the reason far to seek. If there was one story familiar to the people of the early sixteenth century, it was that of Judas Maccabeus sending twelve thousand silver pieces to Jerusalem to have sacrifice made in atonement for the sins of those who had fallen in battle. This passage was continually read as part of Mass for the Dead. And its closing reminder: "Let none doubt that it is a pious thought and a salutary one to pray that the dead may have their sins remitted" taught them how their own devotion in providing Requiems was prefigured in the Old Testament. It was from "the Apocrypha," too, that the Introit and the Gradual for those Masses was taken: "Grant them, O Lord, eternal rest and let light perpetual shine upon them," which, in the Latin: *"Requiem aeternam dona eis, Domine: et lux perpetua luceat eis,"* gave the very name, "Requiem Mass." Thus, whatever might be the rights and wrongs of the scholastic dispute about the relationship of Greek to Hebrew writings (which was later made the ostensible reason for removing the books from the Canon of the Old Testament), there can be no doubt that one powerful reason for the mutilation of the Old Testament was, once more, connected with the destruction of the chantries.

This matter is so far from being academic that only

26

last year (1956) indignant Protestants might read in *The London Times* of Catholic authorities in Spain "suppressing vernacular translations of the Bible" and remark how different it might have been if Spain had had a Reformation. That they were ignorant that Spain, a pioneer of the vernacular Scriptures (the first printed Bible, following many manuscript ones, was published in 1478), was merely protesting against the version supplied by the British and Foreign Bible Society (which, by its constitution, is forbidden to include "the Apocrypha" and thereby suffers, as an Anglican commentator has put it, "the inability to supply complete Bibles") is the measure of their inability to understand the Reformation.

And if, after four centuries, the power of the original propaganda of falsehood is still so strong, what must its effect have been on the ordinary men and women living in England "behind the Iron Curtain" at that time? Again I must content myself, in the short space of an essay, with but one example among many.

At the end of the sixteenth century, among the many bogus "plots" which the Government invented and attributed to Catholics, was one known as "Squire's Plot." The background of it is still not altogether clear, but certain facts are unassailable. Squire, an unsuccessful accountant who lived by his wits, obtained a post in the Royal Stables and confessed, after five hours on the rack, that he had been employed by the Jesuits to poison Queen Elizabeth by smearing a paste of "certain poisonous drugs of which opium was one" on the saddle of her horse.[13] Later he entirely recanted, saying that he had confessed anything he thought would satisfy the Government to relieve himself from torture; and at the gallows itself—knowing that such a course would ensure a vile and lingering death—he protested that his statement under torture was a lie. The story is indeed so preposterous that one cannot but agree with Lingard's judgment that "if Titus Oates had never existed, the history of this ridiculous plot would suffice to show how easily the most absurd fictions obtain credit when the public mind is under the influence of prejudice."[14] And should Lingard, as a Catholic, be deemed to be prejudiced, there is the Protestant Jessop who, after a careful examination of the evidence, asserts: "To me it seems only a monstrous fiction, which the more closely it is looked into the more entirely incredible does it appear."[15] Today, there is no historian, Catholic or Protestant, who would take it seriously, and the only difference of opinion is whether the Government engineered it through all its stages or whether they merely took advantage of and developed an independent lunacy.

What is important is the way in which they used it as propaganda, acting through the parish churches which every citizen had, by law, to attend. No one in England could escape the official version—and that official version was safeguarded against ordinary scepticism by being made a part of the public worship of God. Supplementary prayers were composed and appointed to be used in every church. One of them ended with a reference to the Jesuits as "the hellish Chaplains of Antichrist" and exhorted the Almighty to "let our gracious Queen still reign and rule in despite of Rome and Rheims and Spain and Hell." Another began: "Almighty and Everlasting God, Creator and Governor of all the world, by whom kings do rule and under whose providence they are wonderfully and mightily often times protected from the fearful dangers by which the malice of Satan and his wicked imps do seek to entrap them: We give unto Thy heavenly Majesty most humble and hearty thanks for that it hath pleased Thee of Thine infinite mercy and goodness in Christ Jesu so wonderfully to uphold, deliver and preserve Thine handmaid, our most dread and Sovereign Queen Elizabeth, so many and sundry times from the cruel and bloody treacheries of desperate men who address themselves to all wickedness; and at this time especially, wherein her innocent life was not only attempted but, had it not been for Thy merciful power to prevent it, much endangered by wretched traitors appointed to that purpose, who had performed, as much as in them lay, their wicked designments of impoisoning her Sacred Majesty."

And that there might be no doubt in the minds of the worshippers as to who Satan's wicked imps were and who had attempted the poisoning, the authorities prefaced the Prayer with an "Admonition to the Reader" in which, for the benefit of the preacher, it was laid down: "That which passeth the rest and may be an effectual motive to work in all Christian hearts a sounder devotion of thankfulness to our God and a greater detestation of that blood-sucking Romish Antichrist with his whole swarm of shavelings, was that dreadful attempt of Squire . . . which we, her subjects, do tremble at to remember, utterly to quench the light of Israel and by poison to make away our Sovereign Prince . . . to which horrible practice the said Squire in his voluntary confession, without any torture at all, was first incited and afterwards at several times persuaded, and, appearing somewhat backward, at last encouraged by one Walpole, a cursed Jebusite (Jesuit, I should say)."[16]

With such popularizing of the plot in every church in the land, it is not surprising that eight years later, during the "Gunpowder Plot" trial, the Government spokesman could be sure of making his point when he referred back to Squire who endeavoured "to poison Her Majesty, incited, directed and warranted by Walpole, a Jesuit . . . at whose hands, likewise, after absolution he received the sacrament, as well to put the practice in execution as to keep it secret." What chance had the sixteenth-century Englishman, sixty years after the Reformation started, of understanding the truth? And, one may add, what chance has the ordinary non-Catholic Englishman today, when in State Schools children are instructed, as part of a Protestant "agreed syllabus" of *religious* education, about "Plots (Jesuits) in England against Elizabeth" and taught that the "causes of the Reformation" included "national resentment of Papal interference and exactions" and the fact that "the Bible passed into the hands of the people."[17]

From these few representative instances, Catholics may perhaps better appreciate the very great handicap from which Protestants suffer when they come to consider the story of the Reformation in England. The surprise is not that so few come to the facts of it but that so many have had the pertinacity to unearth the truth, embedded under centuries-hard layers of propaganda, and, in finding it, have found also the courage to admit they have been cozened.

The Existence of Heresy

"It is the peculiarity of England that here the constitutional revolution came before the adoption of a new religion, instead of being accomplished, as elsewhere, by the very impetus of the new theology."[18] Thus the Protestant historian T. M. Parker urbanely epitomizes

31

the situation I have been trying to outline in terms of its practical realities. But because the new Continental theories were a late importation to justify the English Government's already accomplished action, it by no means follows that the prior existence of heresy in Enggland, though negligible in numbers and influence, was unimportant. The conventional description of Wyclif as "the Morning Star of the Reformation" is, in one sense, true enough. The theories underlying Wyclif's Lollardism in the fourteenth and early fifteenth centuries were aspects of that dualism which, in one form or another, may be described as *the* heresy against which the Church has had to struggle from its foundation until today. The essence of dualism, however the emphasis varies, is a denial of the reality of the Incarnation. By asserting the inherent wickedness of "matter," of "the flesh," it continues to separate what Christ united. Implicitly or explicitly, immediately at the centre or peripherally at the fringe of its theology, it denies the first premiss of Christianity—that God became Flesh. Masking itself as Neo-Platonism, Marcionitism and Manichaeism in the early Christian centuries; menacing the structure of European society as Catharism (the Religion of the Pure Ones) in the early Middle Ages and gaining temporary local victories in the later Middle Ages under Hus in Bohemia and Wyclif in England; disrupting seventeenth-century Protestantism in England as Puritanism, and

Catholicism in France as Jansenism; and powerful today in theosophy on the one hand and modernism on the other, it has flourished as the eternal and subtle enemy of the central Christian truth, with which no compromise is possible.

The points of attack are almost as various as its forms, though given the key, they are easy enough to recognize. Sometimes the onslaught is central—on the reality of Christ's human body or of His bodily resurrection, or on His mother as "Mother of God" (or even as a unique human person). Sometimes it is on the sacraments, which are the extension of the Incarnation —a denial of the transubstantiated sacramental Body or a refusal to acknowledge that the spiritual power to forgive sins can be delegated to a human priest. Sometimes it takes extreme forms in which marriage and the procreation of children are denounced as intrinsically evil. Nearly always it allies claims to "the liberty of the spirit" with denunciations of the ordinances of the Visible Church. Usually it regards the Pope as Antichrist, as Presbyterians do today.[19]

In England, the centres of this type of heresy, inherited from the Lollards, were in the industrial "weaver" towns of Essex, in certain districts in Kent and among the Chiltern Hills in Buckinghamshire, as well as in London itself. In the thirteen years before Luther became a religious force, twenty-seven English heretics of this description were burnt and over three hundred pardoned after abjuration and penance.

Though it is true that the new Reformed doctrines found a fruitful seed-bed among these existing heretics and that, in the course of time, English Protestantism became soaked in dualism, the paradox of the English situation was that the Reformers were, in the beginning, every whit as hot against the heretics as were the Catholics.

And the existence of these heretics, given the general, inclusive and slightly misleading name of "Anabaptists," has a distinct bearing on the question of persecution, especially the persecutions under "Bloody Mary." For, as the Anglican historian C. H. Smyth has pointed out, "at least two-thirds" of those who were burnt under Mary would "almost undoubtedly" have been burnt by Edward VI had he survived.[20] Cranmer and the Reformed bishops not only burnt two of their leaders, Joan of Kent and George van Paris, but were scouring Essex and Kent to round up the rank-and-file when the king died. Hooper, himself to suffer under Mary, was most active against "the frenzy of the Anabaptists." Latimer, also a Marian victim, preached vehemently against them. Philpot, another distinguished Protestant martyr, dissociated himself from any doctrinal connection with them and categorically stated, "As for Joan of

Kent, she was a vain woman (I knew her well) and a heretic indeed, well worthy to be burnt."

From Hooper's letter to a fellow Protestant, we know that the "Anabaptist" beliefs were practically identical with those of the mediaeval Cathars; were, that is to say, indeed, *the* heresy. "The Anabaptists," he writes, "give me much trouble with their opinions respecting the incarnation of the Lord; for they deny altogether that Christ was born of the Virgin Mary according to the flesh," and continues to catalogue the well-known and centuries-old tenets of the heresy.[21]

Of the 273 Protestant martyrs burnt in the reign of Queen Mary, only 104 are noticed in any detail by their chronicler and panegyrist, John Foxe, in his famous *Book of Martyrs*. For the other 169 there is nothing but bare entries; and as 111 of them came from Essex and Kent, the strong presumption is that they were "Anabaptists," "whose deaths were no testimony to orthodox Protestantism and of no value against Catholicism."[22] Had Edward VI lived another year, there is every reason to suppose that the responsibility for the "burnings" would have been distributed in the proportions suggested by C. H. Smyth.

The Protestantism which was based on the new Continental theories of Luther and Calvin and Zwingli was another matter altogether. In the ten years before the start of the Reformation in England by Henry VIII's claim to be Head of the Church in 1531, it was mainly an intellectual movement confined to the universities, in particular to Cambridge, where at the White Horse Inn (which, on that account, was nicknamed "Germany") a select group of scholars met to discuss the modern theology and make plans for disseminating it. Here, now in their twenties or early thirties, was a group of men later to become famous as Protestant bishops, Cranmer and Latimer and Ridley, Richard Coxe and Matthew Parker, as well as Tyndale and Coverdale, the translators of the new Bible. Though their ideas were to be eventually imposed on the nation, owing to their convenience to the Government, they had at that point no more *popular* influence than the speculations of an eccentric university avant-garde are apt to have at any time. England, on the eve of the Reformation, was overwhelmingly, if comfortably, Catholic, under a King who, because of his treatise against Luther, had been awarded by the Pope the splendid title of "Defender of the Faith." Almost alone, St. Thomas More saw the shape of the future when he warned his son-in-law that heresy would win such a triumph that Catholics would be grateful if allowed barely to survive, and put on paper the warning: "As the sea will never surround and overwhelm all the land, yet it has eaten it in many places and swallowed whole countries up and made many places sea, which sometime were well-inhabited lands, and has lost part of its own possession again in other places, so, though the faith of Christ shall never be overwhelmed with heresy nor the gates of Hell prevail against Christ's Church, yet, as in some places it winneth in new peoples, so by negligence in some places the old may be lost."[23]

The Crucial Issue

There were thus, doctrinally speaking, two distinct streams of heretical teaching. The older, associated with the "Anabaptists," attacked the central Christian doctrine of the Incarnation (the Unitarians and the Quakers are the most logical of the "Anabaptists" of today) and was abhorrent equally to Catholicism and to "orthodox" Protestantism. The second, embodying "advanced" Continental speculations, professed to keep the main Christian doctrines, but so interpreted them as to destroy their true meaning, and specifically denied beliefs, such as the invocation of saints and the existence of purgatory, which resulted in practices of piety and charity inconvenient to secular policy. But the crucial issue of the Reformation in England was something apart from these. From the beginning it was and to this day for Anglicans it has remained the State's jurisdiction over the Church in spiritual matters—the substitution of the monarch for the Pope.

The Church of England, the new body which the

Reformation brought into existence, allows its members to hold a variety of the heresies which distinguish the different Protestant sects. Extreme modernism, denying both the Virgin Birth and the Resurrection of the Body, flourishes side by side with an "Evangelicalism" which sees the sacraments merely as picturesque symbols and a "Catholicism" which pays the Pope every tribute except obedience. This makes it impossible to condemn, under any specific head, the doctrine of the Church of England, for it has almost as many contradictory doctrines as it has bishops and every incumbent is a law unto himself.

The unique Anglican heresy centres in the single tenet to which all parties subscribe with equal sincerity and which is, indeed, the lynch-pin that prevents the vehicle "whose glory is its inclusiveness" from collapsing in chaos—the assertion that the occupant of the English throne, not the occupant of the See of Peter, is Head of the Church, and that from him or her all spiritual and ecclesiastical jurisdiction flows.

The oath which every Anglican bishop takes today when he does homage to the sovereign on entering into his see runs: "I ... declare that your Majesty is the only Supreme Governor of this your realm in spiritual and ecclesiastical things, as well as in temporal, and that no foreign prelate or potentate has any jurisdiction within this realm; and I acknowledge that I hold the said Bishopric, as well the spiritualities as the temporalities thereof, only of your Majesty." The first part of this is the essential part of the Oath of Supremacy imposed by Henry VIII. Nothing has changed. The issue for which Fisher and More and the first Carthusian martyrs died is, with exactitude, the issue which still separates Anglicanism from Catholicism after four centuries.

And the practical consequences of this initial error remain also. Not only is a new see brought into being by the sovereign through an Order in Council published in the *London Gazette*,[24] but all the so-called Ecclesiastical Courts, though they retain the names and forms of the old spiritual courts (except in so far as they have been altered by Parliament), derive their power directly from the Crown, and all appeal from them must be made to purely secular courts. Public worship on the one hand and the appointment, resignation or dismissal of individual curates on the other, are regulated by Acts of Parliament; and Parliament also controls the public expression of doctrine in the Book of Common Prayer, of which any edition other than that allowed by a Parliamentary majority is illegal.

It follows that the emphasis, if the true perspective is to be preserved, should be placed at the very beginning of the Reformation and on the original "Act of State" itself. For the Supremacy is the distinguishing and enduring issue. Paul III in 1535 excommunicated Henry VIII because he had compelled his subjects, under penalty of death, to hold "that the Bishop of Rome was not the head of the Church and the vicar of Christ and that he himself was the supreme head in the English church."[25] Paul V in 1570 excommunicated Elizabeth I (who had re-enacted Henry's legislation in a new Act of Supremacy) by the Bull, *Regnans in Excelsis,* which opens with a categorical statement of the Christian doctrine: "He Who rules in the Highest and to Whom all power is given both in heaven and earth gave unto one only upon earth, namely to Peter, the chief of the Apostles, and to the Roman Pontiff, the successor of Peter, one Holy, Catholic and Apostolic Church to govern it in the fulness of power. And him He ordained as chief above all nations and kingdoms, to pull down, destroy, dissever, cast off, plant and erect, to combine in the unity of the spirit His faithful people, joined together through mutual charity, and present them whole and sound to his Saviour." It then accuses the English Queen of "unnaturally usurping to herself the place of Supreme Head of the Church in England and the principal jurisdiction and authority thereof."[26] From this original act of defiance and disobedience, the other manifestations of heresy and schism proceed.

It would therefore in any case be of interest to understand what led Henry VIII to take the original decision. But it becomes more than that, it becomes a matter of considerable importance when it is realized that the actual situation involves one of the wildest paradoxes in English history—that St. Thomas More, who was killed by Henry for upholding the papal claims, was converted to a belief in the divine origin of those claims by Henry himself.

Until he read in manuscript the King's book against Luther's denial of the Pope's supremacy, More had thought the Roman primacy was the outcome of a kind of constitutional development. It was Henry's trenchant exposition of the true doctrine which showed More that he must study it more carefully, and in the ten years that followed—1521 to 1531—his researches and discussions convinced him that "the substance of all the holy doctors from St. Ignatius, disciple to St. John the Evangelist, unto our own days" was so "consonant and agreeing" that he could not in conscience deny that the Roman primacy was instituted by God.[27]

It was the King who now denied what he had once written—that no punishment was too great for one who "will not obey the Chief Priest and Supreme Judge upon earth"; that it was impossible to draw distinctions between "Christ's Church" and "the Pope's Church" because the Pope is "Christ's vicar in that Church over which Christ is the Head" and "the whole Church is not only subject to Christ but, for Christ's sake, to Christ's only vicar, the Pope of Rome."[28] And the reason for Henry's change was that "Christ's only vicar" refused him permission to put away his wife and marry his mistress. It was a simple conflict between loyalty and lust. And loyalty lost.

Henry's case for the annulment of his marriage was that the original papal Bull granting him dispensation to marry his brother's widow, Catherine of Aragon (who had been his wife for eighteen years), was faulty. As the Pope who had granted that dispensation had, in addition, issued a second one in the form of a Brief against which no possible argument or objection could be brought, and as, in addition, Catherine's first, short marriage had not been consummated,[29] there was no possibility of the Pope's being able to grant the King's request. And even had an annulment somehow been possible, Henry still could not have married Anne Boleyn, because her sister (and, in all probability, her mother also) had been his mistress, which, by the Canon Law of the time, brought Anne into the same category of forbidden degrees as that on which the King sought release from Catherine.

The essential simplicity of the case has been obscured, not only by Protestant apologists, but by the actual complexity of the arguments, the political moves and the diplomatic delays which marked its course from 1527 when, already in the throes of his passion for Anne Boleyn, Henry first approached the Pope, till 1529, when the case was withdrawn from England for hearing at Rome and Henry, ridding himself of Wolsey, called what is known in history as "the Reformation Parliament" as the first step to taking the matter into his own hands.

At this point there first emerge in opposition the two names which are to recur, epitomizing contrary tendencies, in the story of the Reformation in England—Reginald Pole and Thomas Cranmer. Cranmer, then a forty-one-year-old don at Cambridge, suggested that the King might enlist university opinion on his side. Pole, son of the Countess of Salisbury, the last of the Plantagenets, was at thirty a humanist scholar who had been largely educated abroad, mainly at the King's, his kinsman's, expense. ("I loved and venerated the King," he wrote, "to whose generosity and care I owe my knowledge of letters.")[30] Both Cranmer and Pole were sent abroad to "sound" the European universities. When Pole returned with an unfavourable answer from the French theologians Henry asked his personal opinion and offered him the archbishopric of York, then vacant by Wolsey's death. Pole refused the archbishopric and, with great personal reluctance, gave Henry his own opinion that annulment was impossible. In his letter to the King, he concluded by saying that Henry "stands on the brink of the water and yet may save all his honour; but if he put his foot but one step forward, all his honour is drowned." Finding the conflict between personal affection and gratitude on the one hand and his conscience and theological honesty on the other intolerable, Pole asked Henry's permission, which was eventually granted, to withdraw to the Continent to continue his studies.

When Henry showed Pole's letter and reasoning to Cranmer, Cranmer immediately admitted that it "was written with such wit . . . and of such eloquence that if it were set forth and known to the common people, I suppose it were not possible to persuade them to the contrary."[31] He himself, however, "elegant, graceful and insinuating,"[32] continued to work for Henry, and when, seven months after Pole's leaving England, Warham, the eighty-two-year-old Primate, died, Cranmer succeeded him as Archbishop of Canterbury.

As Henry's chosen instrument for carrying out the annulment in defiance of the Pope, Cranmer's position was from the first equivocal. Quite apart from the fact that he had, during his embassy abroad, "married"[33] the niece of a Continental Reformer and was continuing to live with her in England, he was under the necessity of taking an oath of allegiance that he would "be faithful and obedient to blessed Peter and to the Holy Apostolic Church of Rome and to our Lord, Clement VII, the Lord Pope, and to his successors canonically coming in" and that he would uphold "the rights, dignities, privileges and authority" of the Holy See. Without this, he could not have had the *pallium* or have been consecrated Archbishop. Without it, that is to say, he would have been useless for the King's purpose. But, if he kept his oath, he would be more useless still. So, before taking the oath publicly at his consecration, he swore another, before a notary and witnesses, that he regarded his consecration oath as a mere matter of form. "It was thus with a public act of perjury that the first Protestant Archbishop of Canterbury entered on the duties of his office."[34] Or, as Pole was to put it later: "Other perjurers be wont to break their oath after they have sworn. You broke it before."[35]

Once consecrated and enthroned, Cranmer lost little time. There was need for haste, since Anne Boleyn was pregnant and Henry had already, at some date still unknown, privately married her. In his capacity as Primate of the Church of which, by the Act of 1531, the King was the Head, and secure from interference because of the Act of Appeals, Cranmer on May 23, 1533, officially pronounced Henry's marriage with Catherine of Aragon null and void. Five days later he pronounced the marriage of Henry and Anne Boleyn a true marriage, and four days after that, on Whitsunday, June 1, crowned Anne queen in Westminster Abbey.* On July 4, the Pope quashed Cranmer's judgment, excommunicated him and the bishops associated with him in it, and also pronounced

* Rather less than three years later, when Henry had tired of Anne and was already involved with Jane Seymour, Cranmer obediently pronounced that the marriage between Henry and Anne had never been valid and that the child of it, the future Queen Elizabeth I, was illegitimate.

Henry excommunicate unless, by September, he had left Anne and taken back Catherine. In the March of 1534, the Roman Court, after careful examination, finally refused him an annulment of his marriage, and in England, Parliament obediently completed the machinery of an Erastian state by enacting the abolition of all papal jurisdiction in England and the transference of that jurisdiction to the Crown. As the keystone of this legislation, Henry was now to be recognized as Supreme Head of the Church without the saving clause "as far as the law of Christ allows." All the bishops, except St. John Fisher at Rochester; all the lay officials, except St. Thomas More; all the secular clergy and the religious, except a handful of Carthusians, took the oath in its amended form. During the following year, the protesting proto-martyrs were executed, dying "in and for the faith of the Holy Catholic Church" on the specific and specified issue (for there was then no other) of the supremacy of the Pope.

So the prologue ended. The breach with Rome was effected. The occasion of it was Henry's desire to marry Anne Boleyn, the machinery by which it was brought about was secular legislation imposed by the King acting through a "rubber-stamp" Parliament; the lack of effective opposition to it—as was mentioned at the beginning of this essay but which cannot be too strongly emphasized —was due to the cowardice, self-interest and blindness of the Catholic hierarchy, clergy and laity, in whose defence it can only be said that the issues, as presented to them, were technical rather than religious. "Religion," in the sense in which the term is popularly used, was not in question, though with Cranmer in command, the new Continental doctrines were soon to be brought in to buttress the new English Church the King had created and to justify the revolution now about to begin.

II: THE COURSE OF THE REVOLUTION

THE COURSE OF THE REVOLUTION

The French Ambassador once described Henry VIII as "the most avaricious man in the world" and pointed out that what he expected of his ministers was that they should do "everything to enrich him." At the crisis of his reign, the King was fortunate to find, in Thomas Cromwell, a singularly efficient devotee of Mammon. Humbly born, Cromwell was in his youth a soldier of fortune in Italy where, after some fighting, he became accountant to a merchant-prince in Venice. Subsequently he ran his own business in Antwerp and eventually returned to London where, having made a wealthy marriage, he settled down as a money-lender and solicitor with interests in the cloth trade. He obtained an introduction to Wolsey and by 1525 was managing all his affairs, including the carrying-through of the dissolution of the small monasteries which the Pope had allowed the Cardinal to close so that the proceeds could be used for the foundation of new colleges at Ipswich and Oxford.

In the course of these transactions, Cromwell made himself so well hated that it was generally hoped that he would fall with his patron the Cardinal. He managed, however, by the simple expedient of granting most of Wolsey's property, which he was administering, to Anne Boleyn and her faction, to gain the King's ear. Henry made him a Privy Councillor and Master of the Jewels in 1531, Master of the King's Wards in 1532, Chancellor of the Exchequer in 1533, Master of the Rolls and Secretary to the King (the equivalent of the modern Prime Minister) in 1534, Vicar General and Visitor General of the Monasteries in 1535, Lord Privy Seal and Vicar General for the King for all Spiritual Affairs in 1536, Knight of the Garter in 1537 and Earl of Essex in 1540—in which year, having done his work at home and made the mistake of engineering a German Protestant alliance abroad, he was beheaded.

The method by which Cromwell fulfilled his promise to Henry to make him the richest prince in Christendom was simple enough. Its essence was that, since the King was the Head of the Church, he was the owner of all the Church's land, properties and revenues, if he cared to take them. Cromwell's intentions (though he was not able to carry all of them out) may still be read in his draft in the Public Record Office: "Things to be moved for the King's Highness for an increase and augmentation to be had for maintenance of his most royal estate, and for the defence of the realm, and necessary to be provided for taking away the excess which is the great cause of the abuses in the Church."[36] One example must suffice. A feature of the original anti-papal legislation was the Act of Annates, passed in 1532, which, under the pretence of safeguarding the finances of the English sees, abolished the customary "first fruits" paid to Rome. This payment was made by every new bishop on coming into his see and consisted of a third of the annual revenue. In 1534, the payment of "Annates" was reintroduced, with the difference that they were now to go to the King as Head of the Church; and, in addition, Cromwell proposed that the whole of the first year's income of every new *incumbent* was to be paid to the Crown, as well as a third of the revenues of every Archdeacon.

What Cromwell was able successfully to carry through was the dissolution of the eight hundred or so religious houses and the confiscation of all their possessions. At the beginning of 1535, he sent out his commissioners to compile a detailed inventory of the Church's wealth. "Soon the king knew to a farthing exactly how much the Church owned, what proportion of its revenues came from landed property, from fisheries, from mines, from mills, from urban rents, from the offerings of the faithful, from tithes."[37] There was no secret about what was intended. The Imperial Ambassador put it quite simply when he wrote to his master: "[The King] is very covetous of the goods of the Church, which he already considers his patrimony."[38]

Side by side with the financial commission, Cromwell sent out another, whose purpose was to provide the propaganda excuse for the dissolution by discovering that the monasteries and nunneries were centres of immorality. The four chief Visitors of this enquiry into morals were Layton, Leigh, ap Rice and London. Layton, in his middle thirties, was one of Cromwell's jackals, an ecclesiastical lawyer, an archdeacon "proud that no dirty story could shock him"[39] and determined to make his fortune in the quickest way possible. Leigh, also a lawyer, was the author of the plan so to tighten up monastic discipline that observance of it was impossible. Ap Rice was a scholar and an honest man. London, "one of the vilest men of all this vile time," who had earlier had to do penance for a double adultery, was, at fifty, the eldest of the four. Matthew Parker himself described him as "that fat and filthy prebendary"; it was charged against him that, during the visitation, he solicited the nuns to sin. Eventually even his employers found him impossible, and he was proved guilty of perjury and ended his days in prison.[40]

On the unsupported evidence of these four men—and especially that of Layton—the charges of immorality in the religious houses rest. As it is improbable that, even among Protestants, anyone today takes them seriously, no time need be spent on that aspect of the matter, except to say that no one, on the other hand, pretends that, among the English religious of the time, there were not some who, by their frailties and failings, their lukewarmness and their infections from the world, fell short of their profession. To suppose otherwise would be ingenuous to the point of stupidity. And that a great religious quickening was needed, no one, least of all the Catholics of that day and this, would deny. But such things have nothing to do with Cromwell's campaign against the monasteries. The dissolution was strictly "a financial measure,"[41] and the "moral" slanders a mere necessity of propaganda.

The Great Pillage, once instituted, continued methodically and ruthlessly from the winter of 1537 to the spring of 1540, when the last of the religious houses, Waltham Abbey, was surrendered. The Crown benefited to the extent of at least £20 million (in modern currency), while Cromwell himself, with his nephew Richard (Oliver Cromwell's great-grandfather), managed to secure as their personal share of the loot a dozen abbeys and a total annual *revenue* of nearly £200,000.

The Crown did not retain all the plunder. By the time of Henry VIII's death seven years later—in 1547—two-thirds had already been alienated. Some had gone in gifts to friends and supporters or bribes to potential enemies; more had been exchanged; most had been sold. Nearly sixteen hundred shared in this distribution, which thus created a new landed gentry with a strong vested interest in continuing the Reformation.[42] This too, to a certain extent, conformed with the King's and Cromwell's original intention. To quote again the Imperial Ambassador, writing before the event in the January of 1534: "What the King intends to do is to usurp part of the Church goods and distribute the remainder to noblemen" and, in the September of the same year: "The King will distribute among the gentlemen of the kingdom the greater part of the ecclesiastical revenues to gain their goodwill."[43] The latter forecast was the more accurate. Over half the sales were to people of unknown status, except that they are described as "gentlemen"; yeomen and professional men and the King's direct servants had their opportunity to purchase also. Even so, the nobility did well enough.

These proceedings were not allowed to pass without some opposition on the part of the people of England. The King's actions and the instruments of them, Cranmer and Cromwell, were detested by the country. Rumours were widespread that the attack on the monasteries was to be followed by an attack on the parish churches. On Sunday October 1, 1536, the Vicar of Louth in Lincolnshire preached a sermon, rousing men and women to defend their faith. By the Friday, a "people's army" of ten thousand men occupied Lincoln, but, because it had no effective leader, disintegrated before the army under the Duke of Suffolk which Henry (himself staying in London to superintend the strengthening of the Tower lest Suffolk should be unsuccessful) sent against them with instructions to "with all extremity burn and kill man, woman and child, to the terrible example of all others."[44]

Across the Humber, in Yorkshire, there was, however, a leader. There the revolt started at Beverley on October 8, two days after the occupation of Lincoln, and, with Robert Aske at its head, the Five Wounds of Christ as its banner and the "Pilgrimage of Grace" as its name, it shook the throne. Thirty thousand strong, it included "all the flower of the North"[45] and the King's forces dared not try conclusions with it. Henry was forced to parley, and on his promise to reform the abuses, to pardon the rebels and to hold a Parliament at York (where it would not be overawed by the Court and Cromwell), Aske induced the Pilgrims to return to their homes. "That was the one mistake Aske made . . . he believed the word of a king who was faithless."[46] Henry, once he was strong enough, struck again. There were 216 executions of the leaders, the last to die being Aske himself on July 12, 1537. The Pillage was safeguarded and could now continue.

The two outstanding facts about the Pilgrimage of Grace are that it was entirely representative of the *people* of England and that its motivation was essentially religious. The great council of the Pilgrims included not only the captains of the various "regiments" but representatives chosen from every "wapentake" or parish. Among their thirty demands were, inevitably, the redress of legal, economic and political grievances, but it was the first three that went to the heart of the matter. The first asked for the destruction of the heresies of Wyclif, Hus, Luther and a dozen others; the second asked for the repeal of the Act of Supremacy and the restoration of the Pope's authority in spiritual matters; the third asked for the suppressed abbeys to be restored and the privileges and rights of the Church to be confirmed by Act of Parliament. Aske said that, speaking for himself, "unless the Bishop of Rome was head of the Church in England as heretofore he would die in that quarrel" and the first verse of the Pilgrims' Song embodied the whole matter:

> Christ crucified!
> For thy wounds wide,
> Us commons guide
>   Which pilgrims be
> Through Goddes grace
> For to purchase
> Old wealth and peace
>   Of the spiritualty.

Finally, to quote a modern Protestant historian's judgment on the Pilgrimage: "That its primary motive was discontent with the religious changes already effected and fear of those to come, need not be doubted."[47]

One of the Lincolnshire landholders on the King's side during the first rising was a courtier, Richard Cecil. Originally one of Henry's pages, he had become subsequently Groom of the Wardrobe and Yeoman of the Robes and was now one of the minor favourites who had benefited by the grant of abbey lands. He was Sheriff of Rutland and a power on the Rutland-Northampton-Lincolnshire border, where his own estates at Stamford adjoined those of his wife at Burghley. In the year of the risings, his son, William, who had been educated at Grantham and Stamford, was in his first year at Cambridge, where he was already a member of the "White Horse" set and had made the young Lutheran leaders his chosen friends. His bosom companion was John Cheke, whose mother kept a wine-shop in Cambridge, and whose sister William married (much to his courtier-father's annoyance) as soon as he left the university in 1541. In 1544, Cheke was appointed tutor to Edward, Prince of Wales, and another Protestant friend of William Cecil's, Roger Ascham, made tutor to the Princess Elizabeth. William himself, in the same year, was given, through his father's influence, the lucrative office of profit under the Crown of *custos brevium* in the Court of Common Pleas; and in 1545, his wife having died, he married the daughter of Sir Anthony Cooke, the Governor of the future Edward VI.

Within five years of Thomas Cromwell's death, his

spiritual heir, William Cecil, was thus, at the age of twenty-five, well established at Court and bound by ties of friendship, marriage and self-interest to the extreme Protestant party. There is, that is to say, a continuity in the succession of the three men whose will and genius in fact made the Reformation in England—Thomas Cromwell, William Cecil and William's son, the hunchbacked dwarf, Robert—once the personal act of Henry VIII for his personal reasons had set it in unpredictable motion.

The year of the Pilgrimage of Grace saw also an event which affected another of the main actors in the drama. Early in 1535, Henry had sent messages to Pole in Italy ordering him to write his considered opinions and the reasons for them on the matter of the Supremacy. For eighteen months, Pole had obediently laboured at this and his great, though too prolix, book in the form of a letter to Henry, *Concerning the Unity of the Church*, was at last finished and sent to England, where it arrived a few weeks before the Pilgrimage of Grace.

Pole did not mince matters. He told his cousin plainly that the cause of all the present disasters was Anne Boleyn; he denounced fearlessly Henry's destruction of the unity of the Church, his creation of a national Church and, above all, his assumption of the title "Head of the Church": "Are titles given for nothing, or less than nothing, that men should call you, the robber and persecutor of the Church, the 'Head of the Church'? Your father was a penurious man, but even he founded a few monasteries for the care of the poor; but who can cite any good deed of yours? Pleasure-houses, built for your own gratification, ruined monasteries, wrecked churches, their possessions confiscated to the Crown. . . . You have destroyed your nobles on the most frivolous pretences; you have filled your court with worthless men, to whom you have yielded up everything. But what shall I say of the butcheries; of the dreadful executions which have made England the slaughter-house of the innocent? The holiest and most spotless men, for the new crimes invented by yourself, put to death in the most horrible and unheard-of manner.* The gracious Bishop of Rochester, the unparalleled More, the learned Reynolds, and so many others were victims of your senseless and wicked fury. In their bloody death no torment was spared to them nor any insult to their religion. . . . And *you* are the man who holds that the Pope on account of his moral deficiencies, cannot be Head of the Church!"[48]

Unsurprisingly the King was in no way mollified by the exordium: "Finally I turn to you, Henry, as your friend, your physician, your one-time intimate. I say to you, repent, return, make good your misdeeds. In contrition lies man's hope. I am your Nathan. Be my David."

* He is referring to the hanging, drawing and quartering of the Carthusians and other martyrs.

Henry (additionally infuriated that, exactly a fortnight after he had been forced to appear to grant Aske's demands, the Pope created Pole a Cardinal and appointed him Legate to England) sent a variety of assassins to attempt to murder him. The king then seized and killed two of Pole's brothers on a pretended charge of treason and arrested his aged mother. The proceeding against the men was more political than religious, for if insurrections continued they might form convenient figureheads for a constitutional revolution, since "the weakness of the Tudor claim to the throne, judged by legitimist principles" was that "the Poles, descended from George, Duke of Clarence, Edward IV's brother, were more certain heirs of the Plantagenets than the reigning dynasty."[49] But the action against the mother involved the religious issue. For refusing to acknowledge Henry as Head of the Church, Blessed Margaret Pole, in her seventieth year, was beheaded. When the news was brought to Pole, he said: "Until now I had thought God had given me the grace of being the son of one of the best and most honoured ladies in England. Now He has vouchsafed to honour me still more, by making me the son of a martyr."

The last years of Henry VIII are dominated by the paradox that because his young son Edward, who was to succeed him on his death at the age of fifty-five in 1547, was brought up a Protestant, Cranmer and his Protestant associates at Court were gaining more secular power;

but, at the same time, because the King was troubled by the spread of heresy, their doctrines were being energetically suppressed. The "King's Book," issued in 1543, was, however faulty in some respects, an approximation to Catholic doctrine and represented, in all respects, a strong reaction against the views of Cranmer and his new Protestant bishops. The Act of Six Articles, which was put into full operation after Cromwell's death, enforced belief in transubstantiation, the sufficiency of Communion in one kind, the celibacy of the clergy and the binding effect of vows of chastity, the rightfulness of private Masses* and the necessity of sacramental confession. Though the monasteries and the abbeys and the shrines had gone, the cathedrals and the churches and the majority of the chantries remained. "Catholic doctrines were," to quote a Catholic historian, "largely retained in England after the church in the country, as a result of the repudiation of the Papal jurisdiction, had been withdrawn from the unity of the Church Catholic. In appearance at least, the worship and the daily religious life of the English people must have seemed in 1547 to be pretty much the same as they had been at the beginning of the reign."[50]

If such a thing as Catholicism without the Pope were possible, Henry might be said to have conformed to it.

* Henry, in his will, left money for chantry Masses for his soul.

Four months before his death, Protestant mistranslations of the Bible were once again publicly burnt. In the last few weeks of his life, when extreme pain almost prevented movement, the Protestants round him suggested that he should receive Communion sitting. The King retorted: "If I could throw myself not only on the ground but under the ground, I should not hold myself to have given sufficient honour to the Most Holy Sacrament." Nor need one doubt, perhaps, his ultimate contrition. But because he had denied the claims of Peter, he had destroyed the basis of the faith he continued to profess. "What the King had done was to jettison the foundation principle of historical Christianity. To the consequences of a rejection of this sort, no man can set a limit."[51] And when Henry went to his account and his sceptre fell to a sickly child of nine, controlled politically by his maternal uncles, in search of plunder, and religiously by Cranmer, inveighing against "that great harlot, the pestiferous see of Rome,"[52] all defences went down before the flood of change and the Greater Pillage with its concomitant Books of Common Prayer was loosed on the people of England.

Edward VI's uncles, the Seymour brothers, Edward and Thomas, were at the time respectively forty-one and thirty-nine. The elder became Protector, under the title of the Duke of Somerset; the younger, created Lord Seymour of Sudeley and Lord High Admiral, strengthened his position by marrying Henry VIII's widow, Catherine Parr, and when she died endeavoured to marry Princess Elizabeth. Somerset, to safeguard himself, had his brother executed—a proceeding which alienated any remaining sympathy with him when, in turn, he himself was deposed and executed by his rival, John Dudley, Duke of Northumberland. Northumberland, who controlled the Crown in the last years of the short reign, used the opportunity to change the Tudor succession and get the Crown into his own family by making the young King, with Cranmer's aid, set aside his father's will and nominate Lady Jane Grey, Northumberland's daughter-in-law, as his successor. The plan was, however, defeated by Mary Tudor, to whom the country turned as its rightful Queen on Edward's death; and Northumberland, in his turn, was beheaded.

Spanning the changes, William Cecil remained the constant throughout the reign. Appointed Somerset's private secretary at the beginning of it, he was within a year so powerful that "everything that did not strictly appertain to the official Secretaries of State went through the hands of Cecil,"[53] and even the rising Northumberland was his suitor. In due course Cecil betrayed Somerset to Northumberland and provided his new master with material which only he could supply—a list of fifteen questions to be put to Somerset in the Tower, all of them of a leading character and calculated to compromise the prisoner.[54] Northumberland made Cecil Secretary of State, gave him a knighthood and used him in the drawing-up of the new will disinheriting Mary and Elizabeth, which Cecil and his brother-in-law, John Cheke, both signed. On realizing that Northumberland was doomed, Cecil hastened to betray him to Mary.

By this time, Cecil was not only a very powerful but a very rich man. At thirty-three, he had an income from his property of over £120,000 a year and was able to maintain thirty-six servitors, all wearing his badge and livery. His father had left his own acquisitions to him in Northamptonshire, Rutland, Lincolnshire and elsewhere, and throughout the reign he continued to acquire Church property; and if this was not on the enormous scale of Somerset's and Northumberland's depredations, he had at least the advantage over them of keeping his life to enjoy it. Among other property he was granted the rectory and manor of Wimbledon, a share in the rectory of Godstow and the manors of Berchamstow and Deping and Thetford and Wrangdike and Liddington.

Cecil, too, though he had not Cromwell's title of Vicar General, stood in much the same relation to Cranmer as had his predecessor. The Archbishop not only sent to him in the first place the Protestants he imported from Germany and France to teach Englishmen the new religion, but when the new Prayer Book and the Forty-two Articles of Religion had been agreed upon, he referred them absolutely to Cecil and Cheke, "the two great patrons of the Reformation at Court," before they were submitted to Parliament.

(When Mary became queen, it is perhaps almost unnecessary to add, Cecil became a devout Catholic, "frequenting masses, said litanies with the priest, laboured a pair of great beads [rosaries] which he continually carried, preached to the parishioners in Stamford and asked pardon for his errors in King Edward's time." In an extant Easter book, the first of "the names of them that dwelleth in the pariche of Vembletoun [Wimbledon] that was confessed and received the Sacrament of the Altar" is that of Sir William Cecil.)[55]

The Edwardine pillage was directed to the three remaining sources of the Church's property and income. The Chantries Act, passed in the first year of the reign, confiscated the landed property which was the endowment of the chantries (which were also the schools—for the chantry priest who said the Masses for the souls of the founders was the local schoolmaster). The second plunder was, three years later, of the whole of the plate and valuables of the parish churches—a "mine of wealth," according to Professor Pollard,[56] but impossible fully to estimate. The third, the only thing now left, was the endowments of the bishops' sees, which duly passed into the hands of the politicians.

After the chantry destruction, the first Prayer Book was

issued, with its denial of prayers for the dead and Masses for souls. After the robbery of the churches, the second and more "Protestant" Prayer Book appeared, with its new doctrine denying the reality of the Eucharist and thus demonstrating that the monstrances, ciboria, pyxes and candelabra, already taken to be turned into secular ornaments for the furnishing of the new great houses or melted down "to go where millions now had gone in a short fifteen years,"[57] had been unnecessary and idolatrous luxuries.*

Once more, as in 1536, the people of England rose in revolt. As with the Pilgrimage of Grace, the motive force was religion, but this time the heart of the resistance was in the West.

The imposition of the Prayer Book on the country took place on Whitsunday, June 9, 1549. On June 10, a body of Devonshire peasants, having sampled the service, forced their parish priest to restore the Mass. The news spread and the revolt started. Within ten days a people's army, possibly six thousand strong—the figures are difficult to arrive at accurately—had taken Crediton and were menacing Exeter. Their demands were simple and pointed. They asked for the restoration of the Mass in Latin and the Reservation of the Blessed Sacrament as formerly, Communion in one kind and the return of the old ceremonies, services and images. "We will not re-

* For the chronology of events, see footnote on p. 8.

ceive the new service, because it is but like a Christmas game," they announced, "but we will have our old service of Mattins, Mass, Evensong and procession [i.e. the Litany of Our Lady] in Latin, not in English." They demanded the reimposition of the Six Articles and also declared: "We think it very meet, because he is of the King's blood, the Lord Cardinal Pole should not only have his pardon but also be sent for to Rome and promoted to be of the King's Council."[58]

The royal forces, five thousand strong, with a core of fifteen hundred mercenaries, veteran Italian infantry and German cavalry, finally defeated them outside Exeter. "The killing was indiscriminate; 4000 were shot down or ridden down or hanged before the men of Devon would accept, without enthusiasm, the exquisite prose of Cranmer."[59]

The West was only one of the risings, but in the others —in Hertfordshire, Essex, Rutland, Yorkshire, Worcestershire, Gloucestershire, Wiltshire, Somerset, Hampshire, Sussex, Kent, and, above all, in Norfolk under-Ket—the economic factor played a larger part. The poverty, misery and social upheaval brought about by the dissolution of the monasteries and the confiscation of the chantry lands found in revolt its only and inevitable outlet. All the risings were successfully suppressed by the Government, which proceeded immediately to implement its predetermined policy by the robbery of the churches, the destruction of the altars, and the preparation of the even less welcome edition of the Prayer Book.

If Somerset had had to rely on Continental mercenaries, Cranmer found himself no less dependent on Continental theologians. Even the new Protestant bishops were not sufficiently Protestantized. The Italian Pietro Vermigli (better known as "Peter Martyr") was appointed Regius Professor of Divinity at Oxford, and the Alsatian Martin Bucer given the Divinity Chair at Cambridge. The Pole John Laski, noted for his special vehemence against the Blessed Sacrament, became pastor of the foreign congregations in London and was granted the church of the Austin Friars for a "Temple." Peruçel, the Frenchman, and Michael Florio, the Italian, were also established in London, and Valerand Poullain, with a company of Walloon weavers, was planted at Glastonbury. Bernadine Ochino, once a Capuchin, now a prominent Lutheran, settled in England where (as one of the English bishops complained) "his wife exhibits herself both in dress and appearance as a French lady of rank," and Paul Fagius, specially invited by Cranmer, "since these churches of ours are in great want of learned men," and John ab Ulmis, pupil of Bullinger who had succeeded Zwingli in Zurich, Utenhove, Dryander and Tremelio were among the immigrants summoned to settle the new religion of the English people.

The foreigners were not impressed by the situation

they found. Bucer, even after thirteen months in England, confessed: "Affairs in this country are in a very feeble state. . . . Things for the most part are carried on by means of ordinances which the majority obey very grudgingly." The clergy, he found, remained obstinately unattached to the new religion: "Only a small number have as yet addicted themselves entirely to the kingdom of Christ."[60] Vermigli echoed him. The Protestant ministers themselves shrank from instructing their congregations in beliefs so controversial. "Even our friends are so sparing of their sermons that during the whole of Lent . . . they have not once preached to the people, not even on the day of the commemoration of Christ's death or of His resurrection."[61] Only the Government seemed really to approve of the new order of things. "The ruling powers are virtuous and godly," wrote John ab Ulmis, "but the people have for a long time been most contumacious."[62]

With the Catholics (who were, of course, the vast majority of the nation) confused and cowed and the native Protestants remiss and quarrelling with the foreigners—who themselves could not agree—the situation played into the hands of the Anabaptists, who, Dryander the Spaniard complained, "began openly to show themselves and trouble the Church." The German Micronius was even more definite: "There are Arians, Marcionites, Libertines, Davists and the like monstrosities in great numbers," he wrote in 1550, and by 1551 the cry was "we have need of help in the present difficulties of our affairs" against "sectaries and Epicureans and pseudo-evangelicals . . . and Arians who are beginning to shake our churches with greater violence than ever."[63]

The theological Babel which ensued, with each section of Reformers quarrelling with the other, was in one sense inevitable, because the "right of private judgment" makes Protestantism fissiparous by nature. But the assault on learning which had been proceeding for fifteen years and was now intensified by the destruction of the chantries undoubtedly affected the particular Edwardian situation. A Reformed preacher, in a sermon before the King in 1552, did not scruple to point out: "The decay of students is so great that there are scarce left of every thousand an hundred. There is entering into England more blind ignorance, superstition and infidelity than ever was under Romish bishops. Your realm (which I am sorry to speak) shall become more barbarous than Scythia."[64] The average number of degrees taken at Oxford dropped, during the reign, to 33, compared with the 127 of pre-Dissolution times. The famous university libraries all but vanished. In the Commissioners' visitation of Oxford in 1550 thousands of books were destroyed. Cambridge suffered a slower but even more drastic denudation. Within twenty years there were no more than 177 "cut and mangled" volumes left. The great monastic collections had, of course, been dispersed or destroyed years before. And now the destruction of the chantries extinguished education at the popular level of the "Song Schools" and the "Reading Schools"—the elementary schools of the time—as well as the Grammar Schools. The one, where the incumbent lived "teaching gratis the poor who asked it humbly for the love of God," and the other, which was usually attached to a college of priests, had been a feature of English life for two centuries. Now they were all swept away. By pressure of necessity, a few of them were refounded by the King, but "close on two hundred Grammar Schools . . . existed in England before the reign of Edward VI which were, for the most part, abolished or crippled under him";[65] and there was no Grammar School founded from the beginning of the reign till a hundred years later which had not already existed as a chantry. The Protestant myth, here as elsewhere, is the exact reverse of the truth. Edward VI was not the "Father" of the schools. He was their "Spoiler." As Professor Tawney has put it, "the grammar schools that Edward VI founded are those which King Edward VI did not destroy."[66]

Side by side with the theological chaos, the breakdown of education and the grinding poverty and discontent of the people as a whole, there was, as the reign proceeded, an increasing moral and spiritual squalor. It could not, indeed, be otherwise, and good Catholics and good Protestants alike deplored the fact. To quote Professor Bindoff, the latest Protestant historian of the period: "Wherever we look, from the royal court and the circles of government down to the village and parish, and whatever type of evidence we choose, from Latimer's sweeping denunciations to the detailed facts and figures yielded by the records of the royal and diocesan visitations, we are confronted by the same black picture of irreligion, irreverence and immorality on a truly terrifying scale."[67]

The more orthodox Protestants tended to apportion some of the blame for it to the less orthodox. A leading London citizen, an enthusiastic Lutheran, wrote plainly: "Those very persons who wish to be, so to speak, most evangelical, imitate carnal licentiousness, under the pretext of religion and liberty. Every kind of vice, alas! is rife among them and especially that of adultery and fornication, which they do not consider a sin."

Cranmer did what he could. He drew up a new code, the *Reformatio Legum Ecclesiasticarum*,[68] which enacted the death-penalty for all non-Anglicans and the reimposition of heresy proceedings to discover them; adultery was to be punished by banishment or life imprisonment and blasphemy by burning. Parliament, however, refused to provide facilities for enacting the code—Northumberland, indeed, "rudely bade him stick to his clerical functions"[69]—and by the end of the reign it was still only a draft. He had, however, some success against individual

74

Anabaptists and burnt at Smithfield Joan Bocher in 1550 and George van Paris in 1551, while in 1552 a Government edict allowed him to suppress unlawful sects "newly sprung up in Kent"—presumably the notorious "Family of Love." Armed with at least thus much secular permission, the Archbishop prepared for the final attack on the extremists, though, because of the young King's death, it was left to his successor to carry it out.

If one were in search of a symbol for the six years of Edward, it would be difficult to find a better than the great palace of Somerset House in the Strand, which the Protector Somerset built for himself and which, in the next reign, as the residence of Princess Elizabeth, became, so to speak, the official Protestant headquarters. The first building of Italian architecture in England, it cost him £300,000. To obtain space and materials for it, he demolished St. Mary's Church in the Strand (the site became part of the garden) as well as Chester's Inn and the episcopal houses of Lichfield, Coventry, Worcester and Llandaff. Though this gave him sufficient acreage, the buildings did not yield sufficient stone. He therefore destroyed the church of St. John of Jerusalem, near Smithfield, pulled down the great north cloister of St. Paul's and "the charnel house on the south side thereof, with the chapel, the tombs and monuments therein being all beaten down, the bones of the dead carried into Finsbury Fields and the stone converted into this building."[70]

As this haul was still insufficient, he was on the point of destroying St. Margaret's, Westminster, for the same purpose when he fell from power.

Somerset himself never lived in his new palace, and after his execution in 1552, Edward VI granted it to Princess Elizabeth who, in the month of her brother's death, July, 1553, took up her residence there.

Mary Tudor, when that July at the age of thirty-seven she became the first Queen Regnant of England, did not underrate the difficulties she was bound to encounter as a Catholic sovereign determined to restore the faith as it had been before her father's repudiation of Rome. From the beginning, as she told the Imperial Ambassadors, she "foresaw great inconveniences and that it would be difficult for her to re-establish religion, although her conscience pricked and goaded her so that she greatly wished she could find means to do it."[71] At first, with an optimism which was blind to the realities of the situation, she hoped to effect this by toleration. "I will force no one to go to Mass," she announced, "but I mean to see that those who wish to go shall be free to do so."[72] And she publicly proclaimed that for four months, until the meeting of Parliament in November, she would take no steps to compel anyone to embrace "that religion which God and the world know I have ever professed from my infancy hitherto."[73] Even in November, when the anti-Catholic legislation of Edward VI's reign was repealed, no penalties were provided for disobedience (which makes the Act unique), and its introduction was delayed until December 20. And it was not until the March of 1554, after she had crushed a dangerous rebellion whose avowed purpose was to dethrone her and make Princess Elizabeth queen, that any disciplinary proceedings were instituted. Even Cranmer, whose life in any case was forfeit for high treason for his share in Northumberland's earlier attempt to exclude her from the throne, was merely kept under house-arrest, at Lambeth until, in the September of 1553, his furious denunciation of the Mass as idolatry forced her to act and imprison him in the Tower.

These first eight months of the reign when Mary, both from policy and from preference, was being studiously tolerant were utilized by the Protestant leaders in organizing, under the presiding genius of Sir William Cecil, that brilliantly executed migration to the Continent which has been rightly described by its historian as "one of the most astute manoeuvres that has ever carried a defeated political party to ultimate power."[74]

When the foreign theologians and preachers returned to their homes, they prepared hospitality for their English friends. Particularly at Strasbourg, Emden, Frankfort, Zurich and Aarau, English Protestant communities were founded as centres of training, intrigue and propaganda. It is important, in this matter, to realize that "when the body of Edwardian clergy and 'students' who

77

formed the majority of the first migration left England they had suffered no persecution. Their party had gone out of office; and they were being called upon, in their turn, to accept changes in administrative personnel, for which Edward's reign had established a precedent having less canonical justification than Mary's. A few, certainly, had been imprisoned, but for flagrant acts of sedition, not for heresy. And with unexampled clemency, the greater number of even these political offenders were soon released. . . . A general emigration of Protestants was being preached as early as August 1553; definite steps to carry the plan into execution were taken during September; and the movement was actually in progress during January before any coercive religious measures, even of deprivation, had been enforced by the Marian government."[75]

The movement was financed by Protestant bankers and merchants, of whom forty eventually took part in the exodus, while in London, as early as the December of 1553, there was a directing committee of twenty-six persons of wealth and influence known as "Sustainers." In charge of the scheme abroad were Cecil's brother-in-law, Sir John Cheke; his present father-in-law, Sir Anthony Cooke; two other relations by marriage, Sir Henry Killigrew and Sir Thomas Hoby, and his close associate, Edward VI's Chief Gentleman of the Bedchamber and son-in-law of Lord Chancellor Rich, Sir Thomas Wrothe.

Two of Princess Elizabeth's cousins belonged to the group—John Ashley, husband of her close friend and Lady of the Bedchamber, Kate, and Henry Carey (later Lord Hunsdon), who was used as an emissary at the highest level. Francis Walsingham (later to be Elizabeth's Secretary and Cecil's spymaster), with his three Denny cousins, connected with great Protestant families in the West, also went abroad as a "student," though, as he had been involved in Northumberland's rebellion, his withdrawal was probably mere political prudence. Four Anglican bishops, who had vacated the sees into which they had been "intruded," accompanied the exiles, though of greater ultimate importance was the existence, among the seventy-four clergy and ninety-nine students of divinity, of a group of men, all in their thirties or early forties, who were to become, on their return to England on Mary's death five years later, Archbishops of Canterbury and York and Bishops of London, Winchester, Durham, Bath and Wells, Coventry and Lichfield, Worcester, Hereford, Norwich, Chichester, Salisbury, Lincoln, St. David's and St. Asaph. Several of them were engaged not only in study but in providing the propaganda, books and pamphlets, many of an extremely scurrilous nature,*

* For example, the "exiled" Anglican Bishop of Ossory (later a Prebendary of Canterbury) asks, in a characteristic passage: "What is thy idolatrous Mass and lousy Latin service, thou sosbelly swill-bowl, but the very draught of Antichrist and dregs of

which, with the main "office" at Emden and Cheke as the organizer-in-chief, were taken across the Channel by the "messengers" of the community and disseminated in Kent, East Anglia and London, where the cellars of Somerset House provided a safe and convenient storehouse.

Meanwhile Cecil himself, ostentatious in his Catholicism and contrition, remained in England. With no official position and spending his time between his London house, his country house at Wimbledon and his estates at Burghley, he had safety to act as the necessary liaison with the Protestants at home and, in particular, with Princess Elizabeth. He had, ever since his first appearance in a position of power as Somerset's secretary, paid special attention to Elizabeth, managing her business affairs for her. Now, offering his advice about leases and sales of timber, he could visit her without suspicion. As his biographer has put it: "There was one element of Cecil's activity to which no undue prominence was given, although it was great and continuous—namely, his communications with the Princess Elizabeth. . . . The consummate dexterity exhibited by Elizabeth during the troubled reign of Mary was exactly of a piece with Cecil's own management of his affairs at the same period; and although there is no proof that he guided

the devil?" He describes the Catholic bishops as "impudent maintainers of filthy, stinking whoredom."[76]

her action, it is in evidence that she kept up communication with him on many subjects, and it is in the highest degree probable that she asked his advice on the vital points, upon which on several occasions her very life depended. Camden expressly says that she did so, and he is confirmed by Cecil's household biographer."[77]

Elizabeth was, indeed, Cecil's best pupil as well as the cornerstone of his policy. Her own estimate of her brilliance is immortalized in the two lines she scratched with a diamond on a window-pane

> Much suspected, of me
> Nothing proved can be,

but the plain facts are best preserved in a letter from the Spanish Ambassador in the last year of the reign: "Elizabeth was brought up in the doctrine of the new religion, she was formerly of the French faction, she hates the Queen and has many supporters who are suspect from the point of view of religion. If she succeeds and marries an Englishman, religion will be undermined, everything sacred profaned, Catholics illtreated, churchmen driven out, those monasteries which have been restored will again suffer,* churches will be

*Mary was able to establish the Benedictines at Westminster, the Friars Observant at Greenwich, the Black Friars at St. Bartholomew's and the Carthusians at Sheen, among others. "Yet, in all not a dozen of the great company of abbeys were, even for a short while, re-tenanted by religious; to set up more

destroyed, affairs which had taken a favourable turn will once more be compromised. The heretics have no other intentions. . . . It must not be forgotten that all the disorders that have troubled England during the last four years have aimed at placing its government in Elizabeth's hands sooner than the course of nature would permit, as witness the actions of Peter Carew, the Duke of Suffolk, Courtenay, Dudley, the Frenchman Bertheville, Stafford and others, in which affairs the French and Elizabeth were involved, not to mention Wyatt's rebellion."[78]

"The French and Elizabeth were involved." This sentence gives the clue to the success of the Protestant attack. From the first, international politics bedevilled the Marian situation, for in the duel between Spain and France, England was thrown as a pawn on the Spanish side by the Queen's marriage to Philip of Spain. The unpopularity of the "Spanish Match," culminating in the fierce resentment of Englishmen at being involved on Spain's behalf in an expensive and unsuccessful war in which the last English possession in France was lost, gave a cutting edge to discontent which the religious issue, even with the notorious burnings, could by itself never have provided. "Bloody Mary" is a later inven-

---

was impossible, for, except the Queen and here and there one like the Oxford gentleman who voluntarily restored Church lands, none in England cared to contribute to this revival."[79]

tion; but the Mary who said that men would find "Calais" written on her heart was a comprehensible contemporary.

In another and equally disastrous manner, the marriage to Philip affected the religious situation. One of Mary's first actions was to recall Pole to advise her; but instead of arriving, as he could and should have done, in the July of 1553, he was not allowed in England till the November of 1554. The reason for the delay was that the Emperor, Philip's father, obstructed his journey until Mary was safely married to Philip, lest Mary instead should marry Pole. Such a marriage had, in their youth, been suggested; as Pole had never taken priest's orders, it was possible: and there was no doubt that it would have been as popular in England as the marriage with Philip was unpopular. Pole himself, alone of all Mary's friends and advisors, had counselled her to wed no one but to risk the strangeness of being an unmarried queen regnant and leave the future to God;[80] while to the Pope he had opposed the Spanish marriage in the most uncompromising and informed terms, telling him that he could not "show himself favourable to this union, his knowledge of the national temper convincing him that it was . . . universally odious."[81]

The "ifs of history" is a profitless game, yet, because it is relevant for understanding the true tragedy of Mary's reign, Fr. Philip Hughes's judgment may be quoted: "How far Pole's presence by Mary's side in the first weeks of the reign would have changed her history —and ours—for the better is indeed open to doubt; for no more than Mary was the Cardinal fitted by nature to deal with the varied human vileness that sat around the Queen's council board. But one thing is very certain: the Queen would not then, ever, have sacrificed to Spain either herself or the prospects of restoring the Catholicism still latent in the souls of her people."[82] For the sake of the Hapsburg hegemony of Europe, the Emperor, with all the skill of his thirty years' practice of diplomacy, so worked upon the Papal Court and the English Court that Pole, appointed immediately for the reconciliation of England, was kept idling for sixteen months in Germany, France and the Netherlands, and when on St. Andrew's day, the thirtieth of November 1554, he at last pronounced at Westminster the absolution of England, the situation was beyond retrieving.

"The varied human vileness" is not too strong a description of Mary's councillors. Several of them had been the very men who, in her father's day, had trimmed their sails to his policies; of the laymen, nearly all had made fortunes out of the dissolution of the monasteries; even Gardiner, Bishop of Winchester and Lord Chancellor, the best and most honest of them, had been an opponent of More and Fisher and had publicly upheld the supremacy of the State over the Church.

As at the beginning of the Reformation, so now at the time of its possible reversal, the fault of failure lay with the Catholics themselves. The point has never been put better than in G. K. Chesterton's summary: "Even in this Catholic reign the property of the Catholic Church could not be restored. The very fact that Mary was a fanatic, and yet this act of justice was beyond the wildest dreams of fanaticism—that is the point. The very fact that she was angry enough to commit wrongs for the Church and yet not bold enough to ask for the rights of the Church —that is the test of the time. She was allowed to deprive small men of their lives, she was not allowed to deprive great men of their property—or rather of other people's property. She could punish heresy, she could not punish sacrilege. She was forced into the false position of killing men who had not gone to church and sparing men who had gone there to steal the church ornaments."[83]

It is significant that Cecil was one of the three men chosen to go to Brussels to bring Pole as papal legate back to England, with the warning that the only chance of getting any unanimity in the Council for the return of England to the Faith was for the Pope to dispense "all possessors of any lands or goods of monasteries, colleges or other ecclesiastical houses to hold and enjoy quietly the same, without trouble or scruple." Cecil could certainly advance a variety of cogent reasons—his pages of memoranda on disputed topics were already a hardened habit—and as Pole, with characteristic humor, left him an inkstand in his will, it may be presumed that he did. But neither then nor later did Pole quite give way. He remitted, because he was not in a position to do otherwise, the ecclesiastical pains and penalties to which holders of Church lands were liable, but he did not confirm their title to them.[84] There was left a technical uncertainty to sharpen the prick of conscience. They might hold them without trouble but not altogether without scruple.

Pole's great plan of reform for the English Church, initiated by the summoning of a national synod at the end of 1555, enforced the residence of pastors with their flocks, the instruction of all congregations in the principles of the faith by frequent and intelligent preaching, but even more by example: priests, and particularly bishops, must live frugally, using the greatest part of the revenues for charitable and educational purposes. Colleges were planned where carefully chosen candidates should be the real seed-bed—which is the meaning of seminary—for the future. A new English translation of the New Testament, a catechism and a book of homilies were to be prepared, and an English prayer book for private use was immediately published. Two things defeated Pole—the lack of worthy priests: and Time. Within three years of the meeting of the synod, he and Mary were dead, Elizabeth on the throne, and all the work undone. Even while he was doing it, very many priests resented his reforms and "wished the Cardinal back again in Rome." If one may judge the whole country from the diocese of Lincoln (of which alone we have the account of the metropolitical visitation), the reason would seem to be the great number of priests who had married in the previous reign. When the Anglican settlement allowing a married clergy was re-enacted by Elizabeth, about three-quarters of the Marian priests conformed without resistance.

In one respect only had Pole a success—in his choice of bishops. In 1535 all the Henrician bishops save one, St. John Fisher, had betrayed their Faith to retain their sees; in 1559, when Pole's bishops were under Elizabeth faced with the same choice, all but one resigned their sees rather than betray their faith. This suggests that Pole had at least chosen the right men to carry out his great *Reformatio Angliae*—the true Reformation of the English Church which was never to take place.

That he might the better guide the Reform, Pole, though still only in deacon's orders, allowed himself to be made Archbishop of Canterbury. Cranmer, as a properly consecrated archbishop who had received the *pallium*, could be tried only by the Pope himself. After many delays, he was cited and condemned for heresy by the Pope's proxies, and on March 21, 1556, was burnt at Oxford. On the previous day, in the church of the restored Friars Observant at Greenwich, Pole was ordained priest; but he was unable to go to Canterbury for his consecration and enthronement as archbishop because the Queen wanted him at her side for consultation. A dangerous conspiracy, hatched by the Protestants abroad (and, beyond doubt, implicating Elizabeth), had been discovered. London was to be set on fire in several places and, in the confusion, the exchequer was to be seized and the Queen, if possible, killed.

Five months before Cranmer's execution—in the October of 1555—two other Anglican bishops had suffered a similar fate. They were Ridley, Bishop of London who, thinking Lady Jane Grey's cause had triumphed, had boldly proclaimed Mary a bastard at St. Paul's Cross; and Latimer, the "extremist" Bishop of Worcester, whose character had been well exhibited in his congratulatory letter to Thomas Cromwell on the killing of Pole's family: "Blessed be the God of England whose minister ye be! I heard you once say you would make him [Pole] eat his own heart, which you have now brought to pass, for he must needs eat his own heart and be as heartless as he is graceless."[85]

The lives of Cranmer, Ridley and Latimer were forfeit on the grounds of high treason even if no charges of heresy had been advanced; and of many other eminent Protestants to suffer under Mary it may be said that they died rather for sedition than for heresy (if, indeed, the two could in that particular situation be disentangled) as part of "the panic reply of a social and political order threatened by a force which seemed determined on nothing short of anarchy."[86] But of the humbler and more obscure victims of what a Catholic historian has called "the criminal folly of the Marian repression of heresy,"[87] it may be said that they died for their beliefs with the constancy and simplicity of religious martyrs. It was they who, by their steadfastness and their examples, ensured that Mary who "set herself to burn out 'No Popery' managed to burn it in."[88]

It is true that the orthodox Lutherans described them —for they were Zwinglians or Calvinists—as "the Devil's martyrs."[89] It is true that, had Mary never come to the throne, Cranmer would in all probability have burnt two-thirds of the total of 273 as "Anabaptists."* It is true that the "humanitarianism" which makes the spectacle so shocking to this century was totally absent from that. And it is true that, as one historian has put it, "to obtain a clear view of the Marian persecution is not at all easy: Foxe's *Book of Martyrs*† like a great mountain range lies between us and the facts."[90] But

* See *infra*, pp. 34-35, 74-75.
† Foxe himself was safely abroad, writing his propaganda in Strasbourg, Frankfort and Basle, during the persecution.

none of these things excuses the burnings. They, more than anything else, made England Protestant in emotion, and when, on November 17, 1558, Mary Tudor and Reginald Pole died within a few hours of each other, the Catholic cause was lost.

While Mary was dying, Cecil had drawn up for Elizabeth a document arranging for her accession in details ranging from the closing of the ports to delay the news reaching the Continent to the provision of the right preacher at St. Paul's Cross. He was at once made Secretary of State and continued to rule England, while Elizabeth reigned in it, from that moment until his death in 1598, when he was succeeded by his son Robert whom, for the last ten years of his life, he supervised in the same office.

Elizabeth, whose protestations and practice of Catholicism during Mary's reign had been no less extravagant than Cecil's, threw off the mask within weeks; the Protestants returned, coherent, cohesive and triumphant from abroad, and a Catholic bishop was arrested for protesting against the tone of the sermon of the married priest who had been chosen for St. Paul's Cross.[91] Acts of Supremacy and Uniformity were enacted, after Parliamentary debates whose main interest is that they represented the triumph of the "exiled" Protestant party.

90

The Act of Supremacy, which came into force on May 8, 1559, revived all the anti-papal legislation which Mary had repealed, and also re-enforced the Oath of 1536, acknowledging the sovereign to be "Supreme Governor in all matters ecclesiastical and spiritual." Clergy, judges, all officials and students at universities had to take it on pain of loss of office. Four years later, the penalty was increased to imprisonment and loss of goods for the first and death for the second refusal.

The Act of Uniformity revived, with some slight modifications, the religious settlement of Edward VI, abolishing Catholic doctrine once more and proscribing the Mass. Any clergyman refusing to use the Prayer Book was to lose a year's income and to have six month's imprisonment for the first offence; and life imprisonment for the third. Any layman who criticized the new service was to be heavily fined, and everyone in the country, under pain of a lesser fine, was to attend the Protestant service every Sunday in his parish church. It is of this Act, which came into force on 24 June 1559, that Sir John Neale, the historian of Elizabeth's Parliaments, has written that it "gave the Anglican Church its Prayer Book and made England a Protestant country."[92] Certainly the date of its enactment marks the triumph of the Reformation in England.

The revolution was accomplished. It was thirty years, all but one day, from the morning when at the "trial" of

Catherine of Aragon, as a list of all the bishops was being read out as endorsing King Henry's case, suddenly John Fisher interrupted proceedings with the challenge: "That is not my hand nor seal!"

III: EPILOGUE: THE HALF-CENTURY OF SETTLEMENT

EPILOGUE: THE HALF-CENTURY
OF SETTLEMENT

Elizabeth I was twenty-five when she came to the throne. It was her impending birth which had forced Henry to act so precipitately in appointing Cranmer archbishop to pronounce the Boleyn marriage valid; and she was seven months old when More and Fisher refused the Oath. Her lifetime thus covers all the events which, crowded into three reigns, we have been considering. But her own reign was to last forty-five years. It was, that is to say, twice as long as the period between the Pilgrimage of Grace and her accession.

The seventy-five years which, at the beginning of this essay, I took as defining the period of the Reformation —from the first, guarded Oath of Supremacy in 1531 to the penal legislation imposing a sacramental test in 1606—thus divides up in the ratio of 1:3. The rush of change was followed by the long leisure of settlement. And it is this latter period, when there was continuity not only of policy but of people—of the ruling Cecils, father and son—that made it possible for the revolution to be safeguarded and the new Continental religion to be imposed by the new Spiritual Head of the Anglican Church beyond fear of disturbance. The period is sometimes known as that of the "Catholic counter-attack"; but a more accurate description would be the attempted reconversion of England. For now, at last, the issue was, and was seen to be, the survival of traditional Christian doctrine. With the Elizabethan Acts of Supremacy and Uniformity establishing Erastian Protestantism, the Reformation, with its economic and social revolution accomplished, entered its religious phase.

The Elizabethan Age is of such complexity and importance in the annals of England, its myth, articulated by Shakespeare and Bacon and Sidney and Raleigh and Spenser, so splendid, and its potency—one might even say its contemporary presence—so enduring, that it is difficult to see it, in its strict terms, as the last phase of the English Reformation.

Moreover, the "Elizabethan Settlement" itself presents certain problems and concerns many matters in which historians are still making radical discoveries and, on this account alone, demands individual treatment. Here in this epilogue there can only be suggested to the reader certain lines of thought and the key to the broad lines of the policy.

In the first place, there must be made that act of

historical imagination which allows for certain simple actualities of the situation—as, for example, the *fact* that Elizabeth was illegitimate, having been born to another woman while her father's true wife was still alive, with its consequence that Mary Queen of Scots's claim to the English throne was better than hers; that Philip of Spain, as King-Consort of England, was in the same position after Mary I's death as, later, William of Orange was after Mary II's; that the war with Spain, culminating in the Spanish Armada, was a trade war, provoked by successful English piracy and was not in any sense, "religious";[93] and that the Jesuits were a new and very "modern" order whose founder died only two years before Elizabeth's accession. In the second place, it is important to see the object of Cecilian policy in relation to the means by which it was achieved.

At the beginning, there was a hope of reconciliation with the Holy See. Elizabeth wished to marry Northumberland's son, Robert Dudley, whom she subsequently created Earl of Leicester. Leicester's friend and ally in this matter was Elizabeth's brother-in-law, Philip of Spain. His enemy was Cecil. In the January of 1561, Leicester, through an emissary and with Elizabeth's knowledge, approached Philip, suggesting that, in return for Philip's open approval of the marriage, he would lead in person a delegation to the Council of Trent and thus bring England back into the Catholic fold. Meanwhile, before the King's reply could be considered, Cecil had countered by suggesting a meeting of the Council to consider the proposed marriage. A papal nuncio was already on his way to England, and it was decided that Elizabeth should meet him on the Thames out of London, which would avoid any religious or diplomatic difficulties, and that on St. George's Day, April 23, a great celebration should be held at which both the marriage decision and the consequent concessions to Catholics, blessed by the nuncio, would be announced.

On April 14 Cecil struck. He had been busy preparing the weapon which he and his son after him were to use with consummate skill for the next half century—the fabrication of bogus "Catholic plots." A priest named either Devon or Cox was seized at Gravesend. His courage gave way under torture and he confessed that he was the chaplain of Sir Edward Waldegrave, at whose house he had said Mass daily. He was on his way to Flanders to distribute money in alms amongst the poorer English Catholics there. About the same time, Cecil intercepted a letter from one of the imprisoned Catholic bishops hoping that, through the good offices of the nuncio, he and his fellow sufferers might at last regain their liberty. Even Cecil found it difficult to combine these into a plausible scare of a widespread plot to reestablish Catholicism by force of foreign arms; but by arresting about two hundred Catholics in various parts of the country, he contrived to disseminate sufficient alarm to ensure that when the Council met to discuss the reception of the nuncio, the climate was such that the whole scheme came to nothing. Cecil declared that anyone who voted for the nuncio's reception would be guilty of treason, and by the use of this word, which was to prove so useful to him for the rest of the reign, he ensured that "though many wished the nuncio should be heard, he was in fact refused by the common vote of all." "I was forced to seek byways," Cecil admitted; "when I saw the Romish influence toward, I thought it necessary to dull the Papists' expectation by discovering of certain Mass-mongers and punishing them."[94]

He and his son Robert continued to practise this technique until its culmination in the famous "Gunpowder Plot," forty-four years later, made further experiments unnecessary. The pattern was constant. The objective, from the beginning to the end, was the same—to prevent the reconversion of England. In this first example, the nuncio had to be turned back; later, as the stream of missionaries continued to flow, undeterred by almost certain torture and death, simple priests had to be excluded.

Between William Cecil's plot to ensure the exclusion of the nuncio, with all the possibilities of reconciliation which that visit held, and Robert Cecil's masterpiece, there were twenty or so such plots. Widely differing in detail, they had one feature in common. They were all known to, nursed by and, at the right moment, "discovered" by the Government, which used in the elucidation (as well as, often, in the construction) of them, its spies, forgers, *agents provocateurs* and torturers. One or two of them may have had a genuine foundation in fact, but the more that is known about them, the more completely suspect their authenticity becomes. To quote the Protestant historian Martin Hume (who wrote as long ago as 1901, since when every new fact discovered has confirmed the spuriousness of the plots): "The accusations that have been repeated by nearly every historian from Elizabeth's time to our own of widespread and numerous plots to assassinate the Queen at this period are to a large extent unsupported by serious evidence. . . . Pamphlets and broadsides, professing to give the whole story of the various murder plots, were numerous, and have formed the basis of our historical relations for three centuries; but they were written in nearly every instance with political or party object and, from the nature of the case, were necessarily based upon an imperfect or partial statement of the facts."[95]

There is nothing, objectively speaking, particularly reprehensible about the governmental construction of "plots" to achieve a specific object. It has been a conventional device of all governments from the earliest times till the present day and is a recognized part of

100

non-Christian *realpolitik*. In revolutionary or immediately post-revolutionary situations, it is almost inevitable, and in the sixteenth and seventeenth centuries in England the climate was notably propitious for its use. Cecil would have been a lesser statesman than he was if he had not used it. His problem was two-fold. He had at all costs to prevent the reconversion, which meant, in effect, maintaining what is now called "the Iron Curtain," so that no Catholic missionaries could enter the country. And to do this, he had to enact increasingly severe and stringent anti-Catholic legislation in a country which, if not still overwhelmingly Catholic at heart, had probably no family of which one member at least was not a "recusant." The perpetual "discovery" of "plots," each of which was given the widest possible publicity,* was the most effective way of branding Catholics as a whole as actual traitors and potential murderers and so gaining approval for legislation which otherwise would have been impossible to enforce.

The Ridolfi plot of 1571 facilitated the penal laws of that and the following year; Parry's plot of 1585 those of that year; the Babington plot of 1586 was framed for the purpose of killing Mary Queen of Scots and making palatable the savage economic legislation of 1587; in the nineties there were Polwhele's plot and Collen's plot and Squire's plot, to say nothing of the more important

* As in the case of Squire's Plot, see pp. 27-31 *infra*.

plots of Lopez and of Yorke and Williams. "Public indignation and hatred were in this way constantly kept at fever-heat against a party which was represented as constantly plotting against the life of the Queen."[96]

So in 1571 any person bringing into England "any crosses, pictures, beads" and delivering "the same to any subject of this realm" was, as well as the person to whom they were given, subject to the penalties of Praemunire —that is to say, the confiscation of all his goods and imprisonment or outlawry. In 1581, anyone who made or became a convert to Catholicism was subject to the penalties of high treason—hanging, drawing and quartering—and any persons discussing the succession to the throne were to "be judged as felons and shall suffer the pains of death and forfeit." In 1585, Catholics were forbidden to send their children abroad to receive Catholic education, and any "Jesuit, seminary priest or other ecclesiastical person whatsoever" who came as a missionary was guilty of high treason, to be dealt with accordingly, while anyone who omitted to inform on their whereabouts was to be fined and imprisoned at the Queen's pleasure. In 1587, anyone who did not attend the Anglican church every Sunday was fined (in modern values) £600 a month, which must be paid within six months (at each Easter and Michaelmas) under penalty of the confiscation of "all the goods and two parts of all the lands, tenements etc. of such offender." In 1593 this was tightened, so that those over sixteen absenting themselves from the Anglican service for a month "shall be committed to prison, there to remain without bail or maintenance until they shall conform and yield themselves to come to some church and hear divine service according to her Majesty's laws and statutes," and to prevent the "wicked and seditious persons who terming themselves Catholics and being indeed spies and intelligencers not only for her Majesty's foreign enemies but also for rebellious and traitorous subjects born within her Highness's dominions, and hiding their most detestable and devilish purposes under a false pretext of religion and conscience," from travelling; no recusant was allowed to move more than five miles from his home under pain of confiscation of all his goods, chattels and —for his lifetime—lands. In 1606, after the Gunpowder Plot, a new principle was introduced and every known Catholic was forced to receive the Anglican sacrament in his parish church at least once a year under penalty of fines, beginning at (in modern values) £600 for the first abstention, £1200 for the second and £3600 for every subsequent time. Half the fine went to the Crown; the other half to the informer. The hearing of Mass or the saying of Mass continued to be, as it had been under Elizabeth, punishable by death.[97]

The economic pressures were almost irresistible, and the climate induced by them dictated conformity.

And yet the faith was saved. In the darkest hour, England became once more the Island of Saints. And Edmund Campion, who mourned the loss of its right to that title, was of the number who retrieved it. He was only one of many—young men for the most part—who came as missionaries to their homeland, with a full knowledge of what awaited them if they were discovered by Cecil's men, that their countrymen might still receive the sacraments. For the most part they died, and, without exception, they died for their priesthood. This was, indeed, high treason, because a law had just been enacted making it high treason for a priest to enter the country. Such is the basis of the Protestant claim, then and even sometimes now, that Elizabethan Catholics were punished not for their religion but for treason.

And thus the legend arose that Catholics were what the preamble to the Act of 1593 said they were—rebellious, treacherous hypocrites with alien sympathies—and in 1605 the Gunpowder Plot and the subsequent trials were staged to prove it to loyal, peace-loving Protestants once for all.

The legend still persists, for in spite of its demonstrable and demonstrated falsity, it is to this day repeated, taught and officially insisted on in non-Catholic schools and universities. And it will die only when sufficient numbers of people come to realize what, in cold fact, the Reformation in England was—the imposition of a foreign religion to justify an economic revolution, set in motion by the lust of a bad Catholic king who made himself and his successors the Spiritual Heads of a new State Church.

REFERENCES

1. F. M. Powicke, *The Reformation in England* (New York, Oxford, 1941), p. 1.
2. A. Trevisano, *A Relation . . . of the Island of England, about the Year 1500*, p. 23.
3. *Cambridge History of English Literature,* vol. iii, p. 48.
4. Article XXII of the Church of England.
5. R. H. Tawney, *Religion and the Rise of Capitalism* (New York, Harcourt, 1926), p. 138.
6. For the legislation against Catholics see Statutes printed in G. W. Prothero, *Statutes and Constitutional Documents, 1558-1625*.
7. K. Pickthorn, *Early Tudor Government: Henry VIII* (New York, Macmillan, 1934), p. 201.
8. W. S. Holdsworth, *A History of English Law* (Philadelphia, Saunders, 1923-7), vol. i, p. 589.
9. See Account of Campion's trial in R. Simpson, *Edmund Campion*, pp. 393-442.
10. R. T. Davidson, *Archibald Campbell Tait*, vol. ii, p. 201.
11. Archbishop of Canterbury speaking on 30 January 1951.
12. For various Protestant versions, from Wyclif's to King James's, see *The English Hexapla*.
13. Squire's examination, 19 October 1598: Public Record Office.
14. J. Lingard, *History of England,* vol. vi, p. 714.

15. A. Jessop, *One Generation of a Norfolk House*, p. 321.
16. *Liturgies and Occasional Forms of Prayer set forth in the Reign of Queen Elizabeth*, pp. 682 ff.
17. *Agreed Syllabus of Religious Instruction for Middlesex Schools* (1948), p. 189.
18. T. M. Parker, *The English Reformation to 1558* (New York, Oxford, 1950), p. 7.
19. The "Westminster Confession," to which all Presbyterian ministers have to subscribe, asserts in Article XXV that the Pope is "Antichrist, that man of sin and son of perdition." See H. Bettenson, *Documents of the Christian Church* (in the "World's Classics"), p. 348.
20. C. H. Smyth, *Cranmer and the Reformation under Edward VI* (New York, Macmillan, 1926), p. 3.
21. *Original Letters Relative to the English Reformation*, vol. i, pp. 65, 66.
22. P. Hughes, *The Reformation in England* (New York, Macmillan, 1951), vol. ii, p. 262. (See pp. 255-264 for a detailed analysis of the persecution.)
23. More, *English Works*, p. 921.
24. See, for example, the creation of the See of Chelmsford: *London Gazette*, 23 January 1914: and *Chelmsford Diocesan Year Book*, p. 3.
25. The Bull is printed in the series of documents in Pocock's edition of Burnet's *History of the Reformation in the Church of England*, vol. iv, pp. 318-331.
26. Prothero, *op. cit.*, pp. 195, 196.
27. More's letter to Cromwell 5 March 1534, printed in Rogers, *Correspondence of Sir Thomas More*, p. 498, and reproduced in facsimile, Hughes, *op. cit.*, vol. i, pp. 288, 289.
28. *Miscellaneous Writings of Henry VIII* (ed. Macnamara), p. 128.
29. See, for evidence, G. Mattingly, *Catherine of Aragon*, pp. 49 and 209.

30. Quirini's edition of Pole's Correspondence, vol. i, p. 67.
31. Strype, *Memorials of Cranmer*, vol. ii, pp. 675-679 for the matter (including the contents of Pole's letter).
32. The judgment is Friedmann's, who is as impartial an historian as any on a point which still raises contrary passions (*Anne Boleyn*, vol. i, p. 176). He adds: "An admirable deceiver, he possessed the talent of representing the most infamous deeds in the finest words."
33. Canon law, the only law governing marriage, held null and void, by the mere fact, marriages contracted by those in Holy Orders.
34. G. Culkin, *The English Reformation* (Paternoster, 1954), p. 18.
35. Strype's *Chronicle*, App., 213.
36. Printed in *Calendar of Letters and Papers . . . of the Reign of Henry VIII*, vol. vii, p. 1355.
37. Hughes, *op. cit.*, i, p. 283.
38. Chapuys to Charles V: 11 February 1534 (*Letters and Papers*, vol. vii, p. 45).
39. The character-sketch and career of Layton in Hughes, *op. cit.*, vol. i, p. 284, should be read.
40. London was Warden of New College, Oxford. He died in the Fleet Prison in 1543.
41. Thus the Protestant T. M. Parker, *op. cit.*, p. 95. For an analysis of the financial situation, see F. C. Dietz, "English Government Finance, 1485-1558" (*Illinois Social Studies*, vol. ix).
42. For full statistics see A. Savine, *English Monasteries on the Eve of the Dissolution* and the table, based on Savine, in H. A. L. Fisher, *The Political History of England*, vol. v, pp. 499-501.
43. *Letters and Papers*, vol. vii, pp. 45 and 449.
44. For all documents relevant to the Pilgrimage of Grace see

109

Letters and Papers, vol. xi; and, for a full account, M. H. and R. Dodds, *The Pilgrimage of Grace.*

45. The description is that of the Royal Commander-in-Chief, Norfolk, in a letter to the Council on 29 October.

46. Culkin, *op. cit.,* p. 31.

47. Parker, *op. cit.,* p. 105.

48. From Chapter II of Pole's *De Unitate* (*Pro Unitatis Ecclesiasticae Defensione*) as translated in M. Haile, *The Life of Reginald Pole* (New York, Longmans, 1910) pp. 166, 167.

49. Parker, *op. cit.,* p. 89.

50. Culkin, *op. cit.,* p. 40.

51. Hughes, *op. cit.,* vol i, p. 369.

52. *Writings and Disputations of Thomas Cranmer,* vol. i, p. 614.

53. M. Hume, *The Great Lord Burghley,* p. 17.

54. Written in Cecil's own hand, it is in the Cotton MSS., Titus B. 11.

55. Printed in Tytler, *England under the Reign of Edward VI and Mary . . . Illustrated in a Series of Original Letters,* vol. ii, p. 443. The description of Cecil as a Catholic is Father Persons'.

56. Pollard, *England under Protector Somerset,* p. 269.

57. Hughes, *op. cit.,* vol. ii, p. 159.

58. The demands are printed in Appendix XL of Strype's *Memorials.*

59. H. Belloc, *A History of England* (New York, Putnam, 1925-32), vol. iv, p. 197.

60. *Original Letters,* vol. ii, p. 543.

61. *Ibid.,* p. 546.

62. *Ibid.,* p. 434.

63. *Ibid.,* pp. 560 and 574.

64. Sermon by Bernard Gilpin: see F. O. W. Haweis, *Sketches*

of the Reformation . . . taken from the Contemporary Pulpit, p. 59.

65. A. F. Leach, *English Schools at the Reformation,* p. 5.
66. Tawney, *op. cit.,* p. 143.
67. S. T. Bindoff, *Tudor England* (Pelican Books, 1950), p. 165.
68. For the *Reformatio* see edition by E. Cardwell, *The Reformation of the Ecclesiastical Laws . . .*
69. Pollard, *Political History of England* (New York, Holt, 1912), vol. vi, p. 77.
70. Dugdale, *Monasticon Anglicarum,* quoted in Lee, *Historical Sketches of the Reformation,* p. 403.
71. *Spanish Calendar,* 16 August 1553.
72. *Ibid.,* 2 August 1553.
73. Proclamation of 18 August 1553 printed in Gee and Hardy's *Documents Illustrative of English Church History,* no. lxxii.
74. C. H. Garrett, *The Marian Exiles* (New York, Macmillan, 1938), p. 1. This very important book, which consists for the most part of a carefully documented account of nearly five hundred Protestant refugees and is a monumental piece of research, was published by the Cambridge University Press in 1938 and written by one who approached the question "entirely from the political side," not "as a student of theology or as a religious partisan."
75. *Ibid.,* p. 2.
76. Quoted in S. R. Maitland, *Essays on Subjects Connected with the Reformation,* p. 50.
77. Hume, *op. cit.,* pp. 62 and 64.
78. *Spanish Calendar,* March 1558 (vol. xiii, no. 417). The document consists of notes in the Ambassador's hand for a letter to the King on the succession in England.
79. Prescott, *Spanish Tudor,* p. 412. New edition entitled *Mary Tudor* (New York, Macmillan, 1953).

80. *Venetian Calendar*, 10 February 1554 (vol. v, no. 856).
81. *Ibid.*
82. Hughes, *op. cit.*, vol. ii, p. 186.
83. Chesterton, *A Short History of England* (New York, Dodd, 1917), pp. 153, 154.
84. See J. H. Creehan, "The Return to Obedience," in *The Month*, October 1955; an important "New Judgment on Cardinal Pole" based on hitherto neglected material. As Philip Hughes has put it, "a really good study of Pole's career is still one of the great desiderata of English history." In many ways, he is the key figure of the English Reformation, and in this essay I have, if anything, understated his importance.
85. *Letters and Papers*, vol. xiii, pt. 2, no. 1036.
86. Prescott, *op. cit.*, p. 393.
87. Hughes, *op. cit.*, vol. ii, p. 187.
88. Chesterton, *op. cit.*, p. 153.
89. See N. Pocock, "The Condition of Morals and Religious Belief in the Reign of Edward VI" in *English Historical Review*, vol. x, p. 453.
90. W. Schenk, *Reginald Pole, Cardinal of England* (New York, Longmans, 1950), p. 149.
91. Cotton MSS., Titus C. 10.
92. J. E. Neale, *Elizabeth I and Her Parliaments* (New York, British Book Centre, 1953), p. 51.
93. See Sir John Claughton's Introduction to *State Papers Relating to the Armada* from which may be quoted his dictum that it is quite incorrect "to represent the war as religious: to describe it as a species of crusade instigated by the Pope in order to bring heretical England once more into the fold of the true Church. In reality, nothing can be more inaccurate. . . . The war had its origin in two perfectly clear and wholly mundane causes"—the raids and Elizabeth's encouragement of Spanish rebels.

112

94. For the circumstances and full documentation, see J. H. Pollen, *The English Catholics in the Reign of Elizabeth.*
95. M. Hume, *Treason and Plot,* p. 100.
96. *Ibid.*
97. See Statutes in detail in Prothero, *op. cit.*